AMERICAN INDIANS

OF THE

NORTHEAST

AND

SOUTHEAST

NATIVE AMERICAN TRIBES

AMERICAN INDIANS
OF THE
NORTHEAST
AND
SOUTHEAST

EDITED BY KATHLEEN KUIPER , MANAGER, ARTS AND CULTURE

Educational Publishing

IN ASSOCIATION WITH

EDUCATIONAL SERVICES

974.01
AME

Published in 2012 by Britannica Educational Publishing
(a trademark of Encyclopædia Britannica, Inc.)
in association with Rosen Educational Services, LLC
29 East 21st Street, New York, NY 10010.

Distributed exclusively by Rosen Educational Services.
For a listing of additional Britannica Educational Publishing titles, call toll free (800) 237-9932.

First Edition

Britannica Educational Publishing
Michael I. Levy: Executive Editor
J.E. Luebering: Senior Manager
Marilyn L. Barton: Senior Coordinator, Production Control
Steven Bosco: Director, Editorial Technologies
Lisa S. Braucher: Senior Producer and Data Editor
Yvette Charboneau: Senior Copy Editor
Kathy Nakamura: Manager, Media Acquisition
Kathleen Kuiper: Manager, Arts and Culture

Rosen Educational Services
Jeanne Nagle: Senior Editor
Nelson Sá: Art Director
Cindy Reiman: Photography Manager
Karen Huang: Photo Researcher
Matthew Cauli: Designer, Cover Design
Introduction by Kathleen Kuiper

Library of Congress Cataloging-in-Publication Data

American Indians of the Northeast and Southeast / edited by Kathleen Kuiper.
     p. cm.—(Native American tribes)
"In association with Britannica Educational Publishing, Rosen Educational Services."
Includes bibliographical references and index.
ISBN 978-1-61530-659-6 (library binding)
1. Indians of North America—Northeastern States—History. 2. Indians of North America—Northeastern States—Social life and customs. 3. Indians of North America—Southern States—History. 4. Indians of North America—Southern States—Social life and customs. I. Kuiper, Kathleen.
E78.E2A583 2012
974'.01—dc22

2011016190

Manufactured in the United States of America

On the cover: Modern-day Shawnee man dressed in traditional clothing, surveying the tribes homeland in the Ohio Valley. *Marilyn Angel Wynn/Nativestock.com/Collection Mix: Subjects/Getty Images*

On page x: Seminole women fish with their daughters in Florida in the 1950s. *Willard R. Culver/National Geographic Image Collection/Getty Images*

On pages 1, 27, 63, 79, 102, 119, 143, 144, 146, 149: A replicated Iroquois longhouse, made with the same materials Iroquois-speaking tribes in the Northeast used long ago. *Marilyn Angel Wynn/Nativestock.com/Collection Mix: Subjects/Getty Images*

CONTENTS

121

138

INTRODUCTION

Twenty-eight U.S. states and six Canadian provinces bear names derived from Native American words. In addition, many geographic features—islands (Nantucket), bays (Narragansett), cities (Punxsutawney), rivers (Calumet, Kankakee), and lakes (Huron, Erie)—have aboriginal monikers. But consider the terms given to indigenous peoples of North America themselves. Columbus inaccurately called the native people he encountered Indians, believing that he had found a new passage to India. Likewise, Native "Americans" is not technically correct either, since these societies had been present long before European explorers identified the land as the Americas.

Although such names are technically incorrect, they are used commonly and everyone knows to whom they refer. Therefore, even scientific references to indigenous peoples of the United States and Canada are couched in these terms, with the full awareness of their origins.

This book follows that tradition, examining the Native Americans who first encountered European explorers and settlers, those who inhabited the Northeast and the Southeast portions of the land that became known as North America.

The early days of settlement are remote, but accounts of the contact between Europeans and Native Americans are remarkably vivid, bringing these interactions into sharp focus. Each observer offers a unique perspective. The adventurer John Smith in 1608 offered *A True Relation of Such Occurrences and Accidents of Note as Hath Happened in Virginia*, in which he recorded being saved by Powhatan's daughter Pocahontas. Although his accounts of events have been controversial, his histories—found in *A Description of New England in 1616* and *The General History of Virginia, New England, and the Summer Isles* (1624)—present a fascinating record. Other rewarding accounts exist as well, including Thomas Hariot's 1588 *Brief and True Report* of the Roanoke settlement.

Perhaps the classic work of this time period is the English Puritan separatist William Bradford's *History of Plymouth Plantation, 1620-47.* Bradford is probably best known for providing one of two primary sources on the first Thanksgiving (the second is an account by Edward Winslow). He also recorded the difficulties of the settlers and how the Indians helped to keep them alive. More ominously, he discusses the diseases inadvertently introduced by the Europeans and describes the deaths by smallpox of great numbers of Indians:

> *This spring, also, those Indians that lived about their trading house there fell sick of the smallpox, and died most miserably; for a sorer disease cannot befall them; they fear it more than the plague; for usually they that have this disease have them in abundance, and for want of bedding and linen and other helps, they fall into a lamentable condition, ...*

Bradford continues to detail the bloody agonies of the disease, concluding with the statement "and then being very sore, what with cold and other distempers, they die like rotten sheep." Thus did he foreshadow the disastrous future of native and European interactions.

Before an analysis of indigenous peoples can get under way, anthropologists first determine the boundaries of culture areas, or regions in which specific cultures formed and flourished. From the European settlers' perspective, with some exceptions, the map of American culture areas in the East can be explained in terms of the genesis, development, and expansion of the three principal colonial cultural hearths along the Atlantic seaboard—New England, the South, and the Midland. But this, after all, is the story of the original inhabitants, and most historians of Native America divide the east coast into two culture areas, the Northeast and the Southeast.

The division of North American Indian culture areas was first defined by Clark Wissler, a student of the German-born ethnologist Franz Boas, in his 1917 book *The American Indian*. Wissler used 13 categories to organize his analysis of living cultures (and related, but somewhat different, categories for ancient cultures): food, domesticated animals and transportation, textiles, ceramics, decorative arts, tools, fine arts, social organization, social regulation (such as marriage customs), ritual, mythology, language, and physiology. By working with these constituent components, he could ensure he was comparing similar traits among cultures. He described and mapped the variation he found in each category. The food areas map, for instance, indicated the boundaries within which a particular staple food dominated; he mapped regions, from the Arctic to Tierra del Fuego (in southernmost South America), in which caribou, salmon, bison, maize (corn), cassava (manioc), and guanaco each prevailed in turn.

Although it had been recognized that some traits generally co-occurred (for instance, Native American bison hunters lived in the grasslands and commonly rode horses, wore leather clothes, shunned ceramics, and so forth), Wissler was the first to recognize that patterns of coexisting traits were crucial to an understanding of innovation and diffusion. He demonstrated the close relationship that particular cultural complexes shared with the boundaries of broad environmental zones such as temperate forests, grasslands, and deserts, and combined the cultural and geographic patterns, defining 15 culture areas in North, Central, and South America.

A.L. Kroeber, senior anthropologist at the University of California at Berkeley (1901–46), further developed Wissler's thesis and published the immensely popular

Cultural and Natural Areas of Native North America, which remained in print almost continuously from 1939 until 1976. Kroeber's close colleague at Berkeley, geographer Carl Sauer, and the many students each fostered also promoted the culture area approach to a wide audience.

The concept of the culture area thus became one of the most common lenses through which social scientists, and especially those who studied the Americas, viewed their work. It has continued to be used as a teaching device and a means of ordering data and museum displays in the 21st century. Its fundamental assumptions remain valid, and most social scientists still specialize in just one or two culture areas.

Nevertheless, most social scientists also recognize that the culture areas originally framed by Wissler and others no longer exist as such. In the early 20th century it was almost universally assumed that traditional cultures would be completely assimilated into colonial cultures within a few decades, thus undermining the strict application of comparative anthropology. Indigenous peoples have proven this notion wrong, but the widespread conviction that colonial policies and the large-scale changes they initiated—globalization, urbanization, ecological change, religious-ethnic conflict, and others—would disrupt long-standing ties between specific peoples and places has indeed proved to be the case. Given these cautionary comments, then, herein lies the examination of two culture areas, the Northeast and the Southeast.

The generally accepted boundaries of the Northeast reach from the present-day Canadian provinces of Quebec, Ontario, and the Maritime Provinces (New Brunswick, Nova Scotia, and Prince Edward Island) south to the Ohio River valley (inland) and to North Carolina (on the Atlantic Coast). Except for the Appalachian Mountains, which have some relatively steep slopes, the region's topography is generally rolling. The climate is temperate, precipitation is moderate, and deciduous forest predominates. The Atlantic Ocean defines an extensive coastline, and there is a profusion of rivers and lakes.

The Algonquin, Iroquois, Huron, Wampanoag, Mohican, Mohegan, Ojibwa, Ho-chunk (Winnebago), Sauk, Fox, and Illinois are among the prominent tribes of this culture area. At the time of first contact, most Northeastern peoples engaged in agriculture, and for them the village of a few dozen to a few hundred persons was the most important social and economic unit in daily life. Groups that had access to reliably plentiful wild foods such as wild rice, salmon, or shellfish typically lived in dispersed hamlets of extended families. Several villages or hamlets formed a tribe, and groups of tribes sometimes organized into powerful confederacies. These alliances were often extremely complex political organizations that took their name from the most powerful member tribe, as with the Iroquois Confederacy.

Farming groups relied on cultivated maize, beans, squash, and weedy seed-bearing plants such as *Chenopodium*, a type of amaranth. All peoples of the Northeast hunted animals including deer, elk, moose, waterfowl, turkeys, and fish. They lived in wickiups (wigwams) or longhouses. Though these buildings were of different shapes, both house types consisted of a sapling framework that was covered with rush matting or sheets of bark. Other common aspects of the Northeast culture included the use of dugouts made of the trunks of whole trees and birchbark canoes, clothing made of pelts and deerskins, and a variety of medicine societies that included shamans, prophets, and seers.

The northernmost Southeast region begins at the southern edge of the Northeast culture area and stretches south to the Gulf of Mexico. From east to west it extends from the Atlantic Ocean to an area somewhat west of the Mississippi valley. The characteristic climate is warm temperate in the north and grades to subtropical in the south. Natural features of the Southeast include coastal plains, rolling uplands known as the piedmont, and the southernmost Appalachian Mountains. Of these, the piedmont was most densely populated. The predominant ecosystems were coastal scrub, wetlands, and deciduous forests.

The so-called Five Civilized Tribes—composed of the Cherokee, Choctaw, Chickasaw, Creek, and Seminole—are perhaps the best-known indigenous peoples originally from this region. Other tribes included the Natchez, Caddo, Apalachee, Timucua, and Guale.

The region's economy was primarily agricultural, and social stratification was common. As chiefdoms, most cultures were structured around hereditary classes of elites and commoners, although some groups used hierarchical systems that had additional status levels. Most people were commoners and lived in hamlets located along waterways. Each hamlet was home to an extended family and typically included a few houses and auxiliary structures such as granaries and summer kitchens, surrounded by agricultural plots or fields. These hamlets were usually associated with a town that served as the area's ceremonial and market centre. Towns often included large earthen mounds on which religious structures and the homes of the ruling classes or families were built. Together, each town and its associated hamlets constituted an autonomous political entity. In times of need these groups could unite into confederacies, such as those of the Creek and Choctaw.

In addition to maize, beans, squash, tobacco, and other crops, the people of the Southeast gathered wild plant foods and shellfish, hunted deer and other animals, and fished. House forms varied extensively across the region, including wickiups (wigwams), earth-berm dwellings, and, in the 19th century, chickees (thatched roofs with open walls). The Southeast was also known for its religious iconography, which often included bird themes.

The general characteristics found within the Northeast and Southeast culture areas are discussed in this volume. But it pays to look beyond the facts, giving some thought to what life must have been like for the peoples of North America before the European settlers arrived. One way to accomplish this is to examine other books such as Charles C. Mann's *1491: New Revelations of the Americas Before Columbus* (2005). Also helpful in this regard would be studying the milieu and perspective of native leaders who lived through the experience of settler encroachment in accounts such as *A Sorrow in the Heart: The Life of Tecumseh* by Allan W. Eckert. An even bigger challenge would be to identify the preconceived notions and loaded words in the histories of William Bradford and John Smith (many of which are available online).

That last point brings up an interesting conundrum. Certain beliefs about the indigenous peoples of North America have been around for centuries. These are based on hearsay or the sometimes embellished and exaggerated tales recounting the early days of America. Scholars have questioned the veracity (or accuracy) of portions of Smith's firsthand account, and fictional stories of Indian life, such as James Fenimore Cooper's Leatherstocking Tales, are subject to poetic license. Therefore, in order to truly understand Indians of the Northeast and Southeast, it would be best if readers would check at the door their own preconceived notions regarding the indigenous peoples of these and all other culture areas.

To better study various groups of people, anthropologists in the 20th century delineated contiguous geographic areas wherein native societies shared many cultural traits. Culture areas throughout North America have been subject to various permutations over the years, as Native American communities splintered due to forced relocation or joined forces to strengthen their tribes. Essentially, there are 10 Native American culture areas in North America, including the Northeast.

The Northeast culture area is roughly bounded in the north by the transition from predominantly deciduous forest to the taiga, in the east by the Atlantic Ocean, in the west by the Mississippi River valley, and in the south by an arc from the present-day North Carolina coast northwest to the Ohio River, and thence southwest to its confluence with the Mississippi River. The Northeast culture area comprises a mosaic of temperate forests, meadows, wetlands, waterways, and coastal zones.

European explorers and colonizers of the 16th century noted that the region was occupied by many different groups, each of which was a member of either the Algonquian, Iroquoian, or Siouan language families. As with linguistically related groups elsewhere (e.g., the French, Italian, and Spanish peoples within the Romance language family), each Native American language family comprised a number of distinct peoples. In discussions of indigenous North American peoples, the Northeast and Southeast culture areas are sometimes combined and referred to as the Eastern Woodlands. This term is sometimes confused with that of the Eastern Woodland cultures, which designates a group of prehistoric societies rather than a culture area per se.

TRIBAL TERRITORIES AND GROUPINGS

Generally speaking, the peoples of the Northeast can be grouped according to the languages they spoke: Algonquian and Iroquoian. The only group that provides an exception to this rule is the Ho-Chunk (Winnebago), who spoke a Siouan language.

TRADITIONAL TERRITORIES

The Algonquian-speaking groups were disbursed widely throughout the Northeast culture area. Algonquian language families could be found virtually everywhere in the region except the areas immediately surrounding Lakes Erie and Ontario, some parts of the present-day states of Wisconsin and Minnesota, and a portion of the interior of present-day Virginia and North Carolina. Major speakers of Algonquian languages include the Passamaquoddy, Malecite, Mi'kmaq (Micmac) Abenaki, Penobscot, Pennacook, Massachuset, Nauset, Wampanoag, Narraganset, Niantic, Pequot, Mohegan, Nipmuc, Pocomtuc, Mohican (Mahican), Wappinger, Montauk, Delaware, Powhatan, Ojibwa, Menominee, Sauk, Kickapoo, Miami, Shawnee, and Illinois.

The territory around Lakes Ontario and Erie was controlled by peoples speaking Iroquoian languages, including the Mohawk, Oneida, Onondaga, Cayuga, Seneca, Huron, Tionontati, Neutral, Wenrohronon, Erie, Susquehannock, and Laurentian Iroquois. The Tuscarora,

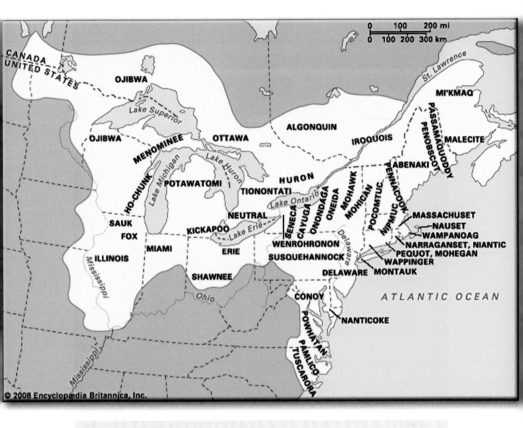

Distribution of Northeast Indians tribes.

who also spoke an Iroquoian language, lived in the coastal hills of present-day North Carolina and Virginia.

Although many Siouan-speaking tribes once lived in the Northeast culture area, only the Ho-Chunk people continue to reside there in large numbers. Most tribes within the Sioux nation moved west in the 16th and 17th centuries, as the effects of colonialism rippled across the continent. Although the Santee Sioux bands had the highest level of conflict with their Ojibwa neighbours, the Teton and Yankton Sioux bands moved the farthest west from their original territory. These bands, as well as most other Siouan-speaking groups, are usually considered to be part of the Plains Indian culture area despite their extended period of residence in the forests.

HO-CHUNK

The Ho-Chunk (also called Ho-Chungra or Winnebago) lived in what is now eastern Wisconsin when encountered in 1634 by French explorer Jean Nicolet. Settled in permanent villages of dome-shaped wickiups (wigwams), the Ho-Chunk cultivated maize (corn), squash, beans, and tobacco. They also participated in communal bison hunts on the prairies to the southwest.

Traditionally, the Ho-Chunk were divided into clans that traced membership through the male line. The clans were organized into two phratries, or kinship groups, of unequal size: the Upper (Air) division contained four clans, the Lower (Earth) division eight. A marriage partner was always drawn from the opposite phratry, never from one's own. Some clans had special functions, such as the adjudication of disputes, and each clan had rites of passage and other customs relating to the well-being of its members.

The major summer ceremonial was the Medicine Dance, which included a secret ceremony for members of the Medicine Dance Society (a religious society open to both men and women) as well as public rituals. The winter feast was a clan ceremonial intended to increase war and hunting powers. The spring Buffalo Dance was a magical ceremonial for calling the bison herds.

In response to the fur trade, the Ho-Chunk began a westerly expansion during the mid-17th century. By the early 19th century they claimed most of what are now southwestern Wisconsin and the northwestern corner of Illinois. This land was ceded to the U.S. government in a series of treaties. The Ho-Chunk were involved in the Black Hawk War of 1832, after which most members of the tribe were removed by the U.S. government to Iowa and later to Missouri and to South Dakota. In 1865 about 1,200 of the Ho-Chunk settled in Nebraska near their friends and allies the Omaha. The larger body of Ho-Chunk later moved back to Wisconsin, where, from 1875, they remained.

Early 21st-century population estimates indicated some 10,000 individuals of Ho-Chunk descent.

THE IROQUOIS CONFEDERACY

From time to time tribes in a particular culture area would form alliances known as confederacies. Sharing resources and combining political and social leadership duties empowered each tribe within a given confederacy. In the Northeast, the most elaborate and powerful political organization was that of the Iroquois Confederacy. A loose coalition of tribes, it originally comprised the Mohawk, Oneida, Onondaga, Cayuga, and Seneca. Later the Tuscarora joined as well. Indigenous traditions hold that the league was formed as a result of the efforts of the leaders Dekanawida and Hiawatha, probably during the 15th or the 16th century.

The original intent of the coalition was to establish peace among the member tribes. One of the most important things it established was a standardized rate for blood money, the compensation paid to the family of a murder victim. Providing compensation for the loss of a family member was a long-standing practice, but, before the confederacy was established, entire tribes could go to war if an offer was deemed inadequate. The fixing of blood money rates prevented such conflicts from occurring within the league, although not between members of the league and other tribes.

Notably, the value of both the victim's life and that of the murderer were part of the compensation, as the murderer had notionally forfeited the right to live by committing such violence. The agreed-upon rate was 10 strings of symbolically important shell beads, or wampum, for the life of a man and 20 strings of wampum for the life of a woman. Thus, the total compensation for murder of a man by a man was 20 strings, of a woman by a woman 40 strings, and so on.

WAMPUM

Tubular shell beads that have been assembled into strings or woven into belts or embroidered ornaments are known as wampum. They were formerly used as a medium of exchange by some North American Indians. The terms *wampum* and *wampumpeag* were initially adopted by English settlers, who derived them from one of the eastern Algonquian languages. Literally translated, *wampumpeag* means "strings of white (shell beads)."

Before contact with white settlers, the Indians used wampum primarily for ceremonial purposes, as a record of an important agreement or treaty, as an object of tribute given by subject tribes, or for gift exchange, the transfer of goods or services that, although regarded as voluntary by the people involved, is part of the expected social behaviour. Its value derived from its ceremonial importance and the skill involved in making it. In the early 17th century wampum came to be used as money in trade between whites and Indians because of a shortage of European currency. When machines were invented in the mid-18th century for mass production of wampum, the resulting inflation stopped its use as money in the eastern United States. Western Indians, however, continued to use it commercially until the mid-19th century.

The Iroquois Confederacy was a league of peace to its members, yet peace within the league also freed the tribes of the confederacy to focus their military power on the conquest of other indigenous groups. Military activities were a primary occupation among men throughout the Northeast, and military honours were the primary gauge of a man's status within many tribes. Raids provided room for expansion as well as captive women and children. Such captives were often adopted into the tribe in order to replace family members lost to death or capture. Captive adult men, however, generally fared less well than women and children. Among the Iroquois Confederacy, other Iroquoian speakers, and perhaps a few Algonquian groups, men taken during raids might be either tortured to death or adopted into the tribe. If the captive had been taken to compensate for a murder, his fate was usually determined by the family of the deceased. If their decision was to torture, the captive tried to avoid crying out, a practice that contributed to the stereotype of the stoicism among indigenous Americans. Among the Iroquois it was not uncommon to close the event by cannibalizing the body, a practice that alienated surrounding tribes.

Although conflicts between the Iroquois Confederacy and neighbouring tribes certainly antedated colonization, it is equally certain that the confederacy increased its raiding activity during the ensuing centuries. This occurred for a number of reasons—some, such as demographic collapse, indirectly promoted violence, while others, such as economic pressures, were direct instigators of conflict. Although it is nearly impossible to completely untangle the ways that these processes interacted, it is useful to consider them both.

Europeans who traveled to the Americas brought with them diseases to which indigenous peoples had no immunity. These new diseases proved much more deadly to Amerindians than they had been to Europeans and ultimately precipitated a pancontinental demographic collapse. The introduced diseases proved especially virulent in the concentrated settlements of the Iroquoians, who began to suffer heavier population losses than their neighbours. In attempting to replace those who had died during epidemics, the tribes of the Iroquois Confederacy seem to have taken kidnapping to unprecedented levels.

Economic disruptions related to the commercialization of animal resources also instigated intertribal conflict. By the early 17th century, trapping had severely depleted the beaver population around the Great Lakes. At that time beaver pelts were the most important commodity in the fur trade economy and could easily be bartered for guns, ammunition, and other goods necessary to ensure a tribe's safety, or even preeminence, in a region. The Iroquois Confederacy occupied some of the more depleted beaver habitat and began a military campaign intended to effect expansion into territory that had not been overhunted.

OTHER CONFEDERACIES AND ALLIANCES

While raiding for expansionist purposes might have differed from raiding intended to take captives, those tribes that were put on the defensive created several alliances to repel confederacy attacks. A prominent example was an alliance known as the Wendat Confederacy, which comprised several Huron bands and the Tionontati. The Wenrohronon and the Neutral tribes also formed loose defensive coalitions. Ultimately, however, these alliances proved ineffective. The Iroquois Confederacy conquered the Wendat in 1648–50, the Neutral in 1651, the Erie in 1656, and the Susquehannock in 1676.

TRADITIONAL SUBSISTENCE AND SETTLEMENT

Geographic location greatly influences how a society lives. Availability of resources in a region dictates everything from diet and housing to the development of self-sustaining communities. Native American communities within the Northeast culture area have reflected the climate and available materials and resources in a region of abundant temperate forests, meadows, wetlands, and waterways.

The traditional diet of Northeast Native Americans consisted of a wide variety of cultivated, hunted, and gathered foods, including maize, beans, squash, deer, fish, waterbirds, leaves, seeds, tubers, berries, roots, nuts, and maple syrup. Maize was generally converted to hominy by soaking the kernels in ashes, removing the hulls, and pounding the remaining mass with a wooden pestle in a mortar hollowed out of a tree trunk. Occasionally, however, the maize was ground between two flat stones.

Rivers in the northern and eastern parts of the culture area had annual runs of anadromous fish such as salmon. In the north people tended to rely more upon fish than on crops as the latter were frequently destroyed by frost. Similarly, groups in the upper Great Lakes relied more upon wild rice (*Zizania aquatica*) than on crops, and

HOMINY

The product of kernels of maize (corn)—either whole or ground—from which the hull and germ have been removed by a process that usually involves a caustic agent is called hominy. It was traditionally prepared by boiling the maize in a dilute lye solution made from wood-ash leachings until the hulls could be easily removed by hand and flushed away with running water. In the modern commercial technique, maize is boiled in dilute sodium hydroxide, and the hulls are removed by the combined action of rotating cylinders and running water.

Wood-ash lye is still often employed in this process to impart calcium to the kernels. Hominy can be made in the home by soaking dried, shelled maize in a baking-soda solution and then removing the hulls.

Hominy is perhaps most familiar in the form of coarsely ground grits, boiled and served with butter, gravy, or syrup for breakfast or shaped into cakes and fried. Grits from white maize are processed into cornflake cereals. Hominy is also sometimes used in brewing and in the manufacture of wallpaper paste.

peoples on the western fringes of the culture area relied more upon hunting the bison that roamed the local tall-grass prairies than on agriculture. On the Atlantic coast and along major inland rivers, shellfish were plentiful and played an important part in the diet.

In contrast, residents of the central and southern parts of the culture area tended to rely quite heavily upon crops, because wild resources such as rice, anadromous fish, shellfish, and bison were unavailable. Notably, the geographic distribution of those areas where domesticated plants were essential mirrors the distribution of Iroquoians, while the Algonquian and Siouan groups generally lived in the areas of enriched wild resources.

This is not to imply that the Algonquians and Siouans did not farm. All the Northeastern tribes were familiar with maize, beans, and squash—often referred to as the "three sisters" for their complementary growing habits, nutritional value, and ease of storage. Fields were created by girdling trees and burning any undergrowth. Fruit and nut trees were not girdled but rather became part of the larger garden or field system. Crops were planted in small mounds or hills about three feet (one metre) across. Maize was planted in the centre of the mound, beans in a ring around the maize, and squash around the beans. As the plants grew, bean runners used the maize stalks as a support, and the broad leaves of the squash plants shaded out weeds and conserved soil moisture. The nitrogen depletion caused by intensive maize production was repaired by the beans' ability to fix nitrogen to the soil, and in combination the plant trio provided a wide complement of proteins and vitamins. Harvested produce was eaten fresh or dried and stored for winter meals, as were wild foods.

The tribes that relied most heavily upon agriculture tended to coalesce into the largest settlements, perhaps because they needed to store and defend the harvest. Large Iroquoian villages, for instance, were protected by as many as three concentric palisades at the time of initial European contact, indicating that these groups were quite concerned about raids from fellow tribes. In contrast, Algonquian and Siouan oral traditions and early European reports indicate that the peoples living in areas with enriched wild food sources such as wild rice or salmon tended to live in relatively smaller and less protected villages and to spend more of their time in dispersed hunting and gathering camps. By the first half of the 17th century, however, nearly every village was ringed by a protective palisade.

Algonquian and Siouan homes were wickiups or wigwams. Iroquoians lived in longhouses. Wickiups were made by driving a number of pointed poles into the ground to make a circular or oval floor plan ranging from 15 to 20 feet (4.5 to 6 metres) in diameter. These poles were tied together with strips of bark and reinforced with other poles tied horizontally to make a dome-shaped framework that was covered with bark, reeds, or woven mats, the type of covering depending on the availability of materials in the area. A single fire in the centre provided heat for cooking and for warmth. Typically, a wickiup would house a single two- or three-generation family, although two close families would occasionally share a home.

Traditional longhouses were also made of a framework of poles covered with bark sheets but were roughly rectangular in floor plan, with a door at either end and an arched roof. In terms of construction, a longhouse was rather like a greatly elongated wickiup. After European contact, longhouse construction techniques changed so that walls were built to remain vertical, rather than to create a roof arch, and were topped with a gable roof. A longhouse was usually some 22 to 23 feet (6 to 7 metres) wide and might be anywhere from 40 to 400 feet (12 to 122 metres) in length depending on the number of families living in it. Interior walls divided longhouses into compartments, and usually one nuclear family would reside in each. A series of hearths was placed down the middle of the structure, with the families on either side of the central walkway sharing the fire in the middle. The average longhouse probably had five fires and 10 families.

CLOTHING

Although housing and the reliance upon agriculture varied from tribe to tribe, clothing was fairly similar throughout the Northeast culture area. The basic item of men's dress was the breechcloth, a strip of soft leather drawn between the legs and held in place by looping it over a belt at the waist. For protection from the cold or while traveling in the forest, leggings—basically, two tubes of leather or fur also attached to the waist belt—were added. A cape or robe of leather or fur was also worn in cold weather. The basic item of women's dress was a skirt, to which might be added leggings tied at the knee and a cape or robe. Both men and women wore moccasins, the soft-soled and heelless shoe adapted, among

Northeast Indian moccasins decorated with quillwork, glass beads, and strips of wool. © Lee Boltin other things, for use with the snowshoe.

Clothing might be decorated with painting, porcupine-quill embroidery, shells, or shell beads. Glass beads, cloth, and ribbons were highly sought after once the fur trade made them available. For special occasions such as feasts and war expeditions, the body might also be decorated with paint and jewelry. Body modification and ornamentation were common. Many individuals had tattoos, especially on the face, long hair was admired and might be greased to

Hair worn in the traditional roach style common to some Northeast Indian nations. Ma-Ka-Tai-Me-She-Kia-Kiah, or Black Hawk, a Saukie Brave, *lithograph by I.T. Bowen's Lithographic Establishment, c. 1838.* Library of Congress, Washington, D.C.

add lustre, and a number of men plucked out some hair and cut the remainder to form roaches (a hairstyle now commonly referred to as a "Mohawk") or other distinctive hairstyles.

TOOLS, IMPLEMENTS, AND LABOUR

Forests of the region provided plentiful lumber. Consequently, wood was the primary production material of most Northeast cultures. Dishes and spoons were made of bark or carved wood. Maize-based potages—a dietary staple—were usually cooked in ceramic pots or birch-bark baskets; hot stones were placed in the latter. Brass pots and kettles were prized for cooking once they became available as trade items.

Wooden dugouts and bark canoes were used for transport on the region's many lakes and streams. Birch bark made the best canoes in terms of the ratio between strength and weight. The forest also provided materials for the frames of snowshoes, which made travel in the winter easier and which were essential in the north. The shafts for bows, arrows, and spears were also made of wood, while points for the arrows and spears were chipped from stone, as were many knives and other sharp-edged implements. A variety of bone tools were also made, primarily for processing animal hides into soft leather. European metal goods became popular replacements for bone tools and stone arrowheads and knives, and indigenous peoples often fashioned the metal from damaged kettles into these familiar tools.

Typically, labour was divided on the basis of gender and age. Grandparents, great-aunts and great-uncles, and older siblings and cousins helped parents care for children from toddlerhood on, teaching them the ways of the group. Women cared for infants, cooked, made clothing and basketry containers, gathered wild plants and shellfish, fished, and made the tools necessary for these tasks. They also planted, weeded, and harvested all crops. In total, women typically grew, gathered, or caught the majority of the food consumed by a group. Men held councils, warred, built houses, hunted, fished, and made the implements they needed for these activities.

TRADITIONAL SOCIAL STRATA

Language and cultural ties were not the only bases for social organization within Northeastern culture areas. In addition to tribes made up of bands (for predominantly mobile groups) or villages (for more sedentary peoples), Native Americans of the Northeast gathered based on kinship. These groups included nuclear families, clans, and groups of clans called moieties or phratries. The intersection of these two organizational structures was not uncommon. One's nuclear family, for instance, was generally part of one's village. Connections among kin often smoothed social interaction at the tribal and intertribal levels.

A band or village was a loosely organized collection of people who occupied a particular locale and who recognized a common identity. Bands tended to be smaller and to live in the resource-enriched parts of the region, while villages tended to be larger and more dependent upon agricultural produce. Each typically had a unique name for itself. A number of what were originally band or village appellations are now thought of as tribal names. In some cases, Europeans conflated the identities of a people, their geographic locale, and their leader, as with the people of the Powhatan confederacy, the village known as Powhatan, and the leader Powhatan. Several bands or villages comprised a tribe, which was also loosely organized and which in many parts of the area was not so much a political or decision-making unit as a group of people who spoke a common language and had similar customs.

Although chieftainships often were inherited, personal ability was the basis for the influence that was exercised by a chief, or sachem. Leaders of various levels gathered frequently for councils, which might include 50 or more individuals. Such gatherings normally opened with prayers and an offering of tobacco to the divine, followed by the smoking of a sacred pipe, or calumet. West

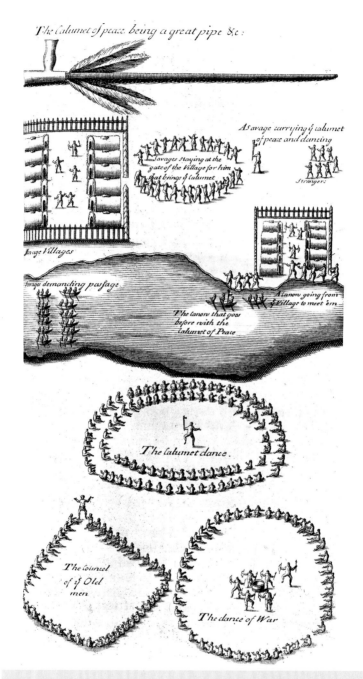

The Calumet of peace, being a great pipe &c:

A savage carrying y calumet of peace and dancing

Savages staying at the gate of the Village for him that brings y calumet

Strangers

Savage Villages

Savages demanding passage

A canow going from y Village to meet 'em

The canow that goes before with the calumet of Peace

The calumet dance.

The councel of y Old men

The dance of War

Stages in the calumet (sacred pipe) ceremony, engraving from a watercolour by John White, c. 1585. Library of Congress, Washington, D.C.

and south of the Great Lakes, this practice was elaborated into the calumet ceremony, and it is from this custom that phrases such as "sharing the peace pipe" are derived.

Persuasion was an important skill for leaders because most communities used a consensus model for decision making. Issues were discussed until there was broad agreement on a course of action. Any dissidents would either leave the group or continue to express their opposition until a change was made. In either case, the effectiveness of the community would be weakened. As a result, oratory was highly valued and developed into a fine art. Even in English translations, the power of Northeast Indian

CALUMET

Also called the peace pipe or the sacred pipe, the calumet is one of the central ceremonial objects of the Northeast Indians as well as the Plains Indians. It was an object of profound veneration that was smoked on ceremonial occasions. Many Native Americans continued to venerate the calumet in the early 21st century.

The sacred pipe was revered as a holy object, and the sacrament of smoking was employed as a major means of communication between humans and sacred beings. The narcotic effect of tobacco and the symbolism of the indrawn and ascending smoke affirmed that such communication took place. The pipe itself was a symbolic microcosm. Its parts, its colours, and the motifs used in decorating it each corresponded to essential parts of the indigenous universe. The pipe was smoked in personal prayer and during collective rituals, and both of these uses commonly began with invocations to the six directions: east, south, west, north, skyward, and earthward. Among some tribes such as the Pawnee, Omaha, and Crow, complex pipe dances were developed that presented smoke offerings to the Almighty on behalf of the entire community.

oratory is evident. Speech making served as a means of ascertaining the diversity of opinion within the group and the manner in which consensus could be reached, for commonly each speaker summarized the opinions previously expressed before offering his own.

CLANS AND KINSHIP

Arguably the most important and stable social group in the Northeast were the clans, which served to divide individual communities into smaller cooperating units. Clans also were a means for uniting people from different villages or bands. Members of a clan had certain obligations toward one another, such as providing hospitality to visitors of the same clan, regardless of tribal or community affiliations.

Clan names often referred to an animal. The Seneca clans, for example, were called Turtle, Bear, Beaver, Wolf, Snipe, Hawk, Deer, and Heron. The animal, or totem, had a special relationship to the members of its clan. Indeed, the word *totem* was adopted into English from an Ojibwa word denoting the close and mutually protective relationship one has with a sister or brother. Members of a clan considered themselves to be related whether or not a definitive genetic relationship could be traced.

Because they represented groups of kin, clans were exogamous, or out-marrying, throughout the Northeast. Ideal marriage partners were often drawn from a specific clan that was seen as the complement of one's own. Some tribes also grouped clans into larger units called moieties (when the clans were evenly distributed) or phratries (when the clans were unevenly distributed). These larger groups had reciprocal obligations. Among many Iroquoians, for example, an important moiety responsibility was to bury the dead of the opposite group.

Among the Iroquoians and the Delaware, clans were matrilineal (sibs). A child was automatically a member of the mother's clan. Patrilineal clans (gentes) were found among the Ho-Chunk and many other upper Great Lakes Algonquian tribes. A child in these tribes was a member of the father's clan.

Thus, an Iroquois child whose father belonged to the Wolf clan and whose mother belonged to the Turtle clan was a member of the Turtle clan. Further, the child could not marry (without being accused of committing incest) any other members of the Turtle clan. Membership in a clan was for life. It did not change upon marriage. Because clan affiliation was so important in structuring community life, those who were born outside the system and were later adopted into a tribe were also adopted into a clan of that tribe.

Clan membership was an important stabilizing device within native societies, as divorce and deaths from battle, childbirth, accident, and illness could change one's fortunes quite precipitously. A clan was responsible for the well-being of its members and ensured that those least able to provide for themselves—an orphaned child, an elder whose children had died or been killed, a widow or widower with several young children—were cared for. In longhouse societies, the enormous houses, each of which was essentially a subset of a specific clan, would often bear these responsibilities.

Each clan owned a number of names, and a newborn child was given a name that was not currently in use. A name would fall out of use when its owner died or took a new name because of a life-changing event. Certain names carried special responsibilities, such as those belonging to the chiefs of the Iroquois Confederacy. When one of those leaders died, the women of his clan decided on a successor who was a member of the same clan. If the successor was approved by the other chiefs, he was given the name of the deceased chief in a condolence ceremony that "raised up" and resuscitated the decedent by giving his name to the successor.

BELIEF SYSTEMS AND SPIRITUALITY

Native American religious traditions are not analogous to Western concepts of religion. Rather than focus on the relationship between humans and the divine, indigenous religions tend to concern themselves more with degrees of sacredness. Everyone and everything is spirit-filled, though not equally.

Animism pervaded many aspects of life for the Northeastern tribes, although it was expressed in a wide variety of ways. Among many upper Great Lakes tribes, each clan owned a bundle of sacred objects. In aggregate the objects in the bundle were seen as spirit beings that were in some sense alive. The clan was responsible for performing the rituals that insured those beings' health and beneficence. The Iroquois had no comparable clan ceremonies. Rather, a significant part of their ritual life centred on ceremonies in recognition of foods as they matured. These rituals included festivals celebrating the maple, strawberry, bean, and green corn harvests, as well as a midwinter ceremony.

Medicine societies, so termed because one of their important functions was curing and because their membership consisted of individuals who had undergone such cures, were also important. Typically their practices combined the use of medicinal plants with what would now be considered psychiatric care or psychological support. The most famous medicine society among the upper Great Lakes Algonquians was the Midewiwin, or Grand Medicine Society, whose elaborate annual or semiannual meetings included the performance of various magical feats. Of the various Iroquois medicine societies, the False Face Society is perhaps best known. The wooden masks worn by members of this society during their rituals were carved from living trees. The masks were believed to be powerful living entities capable of curing the sick when properly cared for or of causing great harm when treated disrespectfully. False Face masks were once commonly found exhibited in museums and pictured in books on Native American art. By the early 21st century, however, many tribes preferred to remove their masks from the public eye as a mark of respect for the sacred.

Not all curing was performed by members of medicine societies. Certain individuals—often termed medicine men, shamans, or powwows (a term that has changed meaning over time)—had the power to cure, a power that was often indicated in a vision or dream. Dreams were especially important, because they indicated not only the causes of illness and an individual's power to cure but also the means of maintaining good fortune in various aspects of life. So much attention was paid to dreams that among some peoples a mother asked her children each morning if they had dreamed in order to teach them to cultivate and attend to these experiences. Dreams could also influence the decisions of councils. Although boys might undertake a vision quest (particularly around the time of puberty), this was not as important in the Northeast as it was among the Plains Indians.

The reliance on dreams should not be interpreted as an indication that these people lived in a fantasy world. Because their cultures placed great emphasis on self-reliance and individual competence, attention to the content of dreams provided a means of understanding oneself and of bringing to consciousness knowledge stored in the unconscious, including knowledge as to where one's greatest abilities lay. Dreams and visions might indicate whether one had special ability in warfare, hunting, and other such activities.

INTERACTION WITH EUROPEAN SETTLERS

Indigenous people of the Northeast culture area entered into a relationship with the Europeans who landed on North American shores that proved to be both beneficial and harmful. The Native Americans welcomed manufactured goods brought over by colonizers, but were unprepared to weather several new and deadly diseases. For example, the first epidemic recorded in New England took place in 1616–17; the disease responsible was believed to be smallpox. No census figures existed for Native Americans at this time, so the number of individuals who perished is difficult to discern with any degree of accuracy. Historically, however, the mortality rates for populations experiencing smallpox for the first time have ranged from 20 percent to 90 percent. The mortality rates appear to have been quite high in this case, as the Puritans who landed at Plymouth in 1620 remarked upon the large number of abandoned villages near their settlement. They interpreted this obvious and recent depopulation of the region as a sign of divine favour—believing that God had used the epidemic to rid the area of indigenous nonbelievers who would have hindered Puritan expansion.

The extensive trade that developed between Northeastern peoples and the French, English, and Dutch

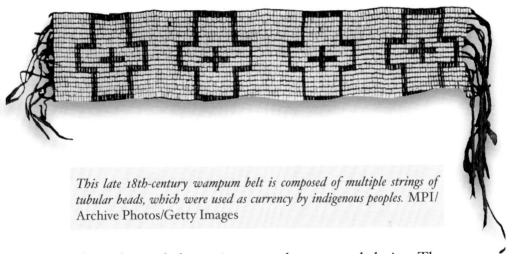

This late 18th-century wampum belt is composed of multiple strings of tubular beads, which were used as currency by indigenous peoples. MPI/ Archive Photos/Getty Images

who colonized the region rested on mutual desire. The Europeans desired furs, especially beaver fur, as the under-coat of a beaver pelt could be processed into a strong felt that was used in making hats. The Northeastern peoples desired objects such as guns, brass pots and kettles, metal needles and fishhooks, glass beads, and cloth.

The colonizers soon discovered the value of wampum and established workshops to mass-produce the material on Long Island and in present-day New Jersey. Wampum was used symbolically as blood money, for jewelry and gifts, and as a mnemonic for significant occasions. Important messages, for instance, were accompanied by strings of wampum that had been fashioned using colours or designs that referred symbolically to the communication's content. The making of treaties likewise involved the exchange of wampum belts to confirm the sincerity of the parties and to symbolically record the agreement. Belts or strings of wampum were also used on other political and religious occasions and kept as reminders of those events. Because it was valuable, wampum became a medium of exchange not only between Indians and traders but also among the colonists. Because the coinage in common use in the colonies was already diverse, including Spanish, Portuguese, French, and Dutch coins as well as English ones, the adoption of wampum as another medium of exchange was an easy matter. Wampum, however, was not used as money before European contact.

The initial European settlement clung to the Atlantic coast—the sea provided the lifeline to the European homeland that the colonists needed—and thus coastal groups were first affected by the newcomers' desire for land. They were ill equipped to counter the invasion. Not only were their numbers relatively small (and made even smaller by the epidemics), but their political organization was not of the kind that easily led to unified action of numbers of men. Friction with the colonists did occasionally erupt, however, as in the Pequot War (1637) and King Philip's War (1675–76). Such resistance could not be maintained for long, however, and indigenous peoples began to adopt European ways as a means of survival. This often involved the acceptance and practice of Christianity. Some missionaries were especially influential. John Eliot, for example, accomplished the monumental task of translating the Bible into Algonquian, publishing the translation in two volumes that appeared in 1661 and 1663.

The Iroquoians fared somewhat better than the coastal Algonquians. In the 17th and 18th centuries, their inland location protected them from European settlement, although part of their eastern territory was colonized. In addition, European traders wished to retain the Iroquoians' services as middlemen who would take the risks associated with transporting manufactured goods and furs over long distances. The Iroquoians understood their positional advantage and engaged in both war and diplomacy to maintain their grip on the region. Their power was finally broken during the American Revolution, when George Washington, aware of the alliance of a number of Iroquoian tribes with the British, sent a punitive expedition into what is now upstate New York. After the revolution, many of these peoples moved to Canada. Others remained in New York state, and some (predominantly Oneida) moved to present-day Wisconsin.

Like native peoples farther east, those of the upper Great Lakes area were greatly affected by the fur trade. The French established a series of trading posts there, and the English challenged them for control of the area. Indians from the east, such as the Delaware, Ottawa, and Shawnee, drifted into the area seeking furs and land. The result was a series of wars and skirmishes involving various combinations of the tribes, the English, and the French. In the 18th and 19th centuries, several prophets attempted to revitalize indigenous culture, and a series of chiefs worked to unite various tribes for the purposes of war. Notable among these were Pontiac (Ottawa), Little Turtle (Miami), Tecumseh and his brother the Prophet (Shawnee), Keokuk (Sauk), and Black Hawk (Sauk).

Eventually the tribes entered into treaty relations with the governments of the United States or Canada, although the terms of these agreements were generally quite unfavourable to the tribes. Despite heroic efforts to protect their homelands, all of the Northeastern peoples that survived the early colonial period had been either moved to far-flung reservations or disenfranchised of their land by the end of the 19th century.

Despite having been removed to reservations distant from their original homes—or, conversely, being forced to partition communally owned tribal land into private holdings in order to retain title thereof (thus losing tribal status)—many of the Northeastern tribes persisted in having active tribal governments and councils and in engaging in a variety of traditional cultural activities. These actions were important as the tribes dealt with a variety of governmental policies during the 20th century, including urban relocation programs and termination, a policy that removed federal recognition from tribes. They were also crucial in the creation of a variety of tribal development projects that include timber mills, manufacturing centres, and casinos. By the late 20th and early 21st centuries, many groups that had lost tribal status had successfully petitioned the U.S. government to reinstitute their sovereignty. For instance, the Menominee of Wisconsin represented one of the first tribes to be reinstated (1973) after termination, while the Mashpee Wampanoag of Massachusetts, long declared "extinct," were granted federal acknowledgement of tribal status in 2007.

Algonquian languages are or were spoken in Canada, New England, the Atlantic coastal region southward to North Carolina, and the Great Lakes region and surrounding areas westward to the Rocky Mountains. The speakers of those languages are represented by the following groups.

ABENAKI

The Abenaki (Abnaki, or Wabanaki) united with other tribes in the 17th century to furnish mutual protection against the Iroquois Confederacy. The name refers to their location "toward the dawn." In its earliest known form, the Abenaki Confederacy consisted of tribes or bands living east and northeast of present-day New York state, including Abenaki, Passamaquoddy and Penobscot in present-day Maine, Malecite and Mi'kmaq (Micmac) in present-day Maritime Provinces, and Cowasuck, Sokoki, and others in present-day Vermont and New Hampshire. Later the confederacy included some tribes as far south as present-day Delaware.

Traditional Abenaki social organization consisted of relatively small kin-based bands led by a civil chief who advised the group and facilitated consensus-based decision making. There was usually a separate war chief. A general council of all adult men and women decided matters relating to war. A smaller council of chiefs and representatives from each family decided other questions of importance to the group. In order to cement relations between bands and with other tribes, the Abenaki engaged in a form of institutionalized comradeship that united two men for life in ritual brotherhood.

The Abenaki engaged in a diversified economy that included hunting, fishing, horticulture, and gathering wild plant foods. The proportion of each activity varied depending on a given band's proximity to the Atlantic coast. Game was taken in snares and traps and by bow and arrow and could include marine mammals such as seals and dolphins. Fishing was undertaken in fresh and salt water. Maize (corn), beans, and squash were grown throughout the tribe's home territory, albeit more intensively in its milder southern reaches. Berries, nuts, mushrooms, maple syrup, and a variety of medicinal plants were among the wild plant foods exploited by the tribe. The typical Abenaki dwelling was the birch-bark-covered wickiup occupied by several families. The birch-bark canoe was in general use for transportation.

The Abenaki interacted with a variety of European visitors during the 16th century. At that time, French, Basque, and English fishermen routinely traversed the North Atlantic to access the great schools of fish found on the Grand Banks. Contact with Europeans exposed Native Americans to Old World diseases for which they had no immunity, eventually depleting Abenaki populations.

As the French and English colonial systems developed in the 17th century, the Abenaki became involved in the fur trade, exchanging beaver and other pelts for imported goods such as metal tools and glass beads. The Abenaki were heavily missionized by French Jesuits in the late 1600s. As a result of this influence, the Abenaki allied with the French against the English in the colonizers' competition for indigenous trade and territory. Severe defeats in 1724 and 1725 again reduced the tribe's numbers. Most withdrew to Canada, eventually settling at Saint-François-du-Lac in Quebec.

Abenaki descendants numbered some 8,000 individuals in the early 21st century.

ALGONQUIN

The densely forested regions of present-day Quebec and Ontario, Can., were originally home to the Algonquin tribe of Native Americans, composed of closely related Algonquian-speaking bands. The tribe should be differentiated from the Algonquian language family, a much larger entity composed of at least 24 tribes of Northeast and Plains Indians.

Sketch of the Algonquin village of Pomeiock, near present-day Gibbs Creek, N.C., showing wickiups and longhouses inside a protective palisade, c. 1585; in the British Museum, London. Photos.com/Jupiterimages

Traditionally, Algonquin people shared many cultural traits with the tribes flanking them on the east, the Innu, and with the Ojibwa to the west. Before colonization by the French, Dutch, and English, the Algonquin were probably organized in bands of patrilineal extended families. Each band resided in a semipermanent longhouse village during the summer, tending gardens of maize (corn), fishing, and collecting wild plant foods. During the winter, bands dispersed across the landscape to hunt terrestrial mammals. In the spring, some Algonquin bands tapped maple trees to make syrup. Military activities, particularly skirmishes with warriors from the Iroquois Confederacy, occurred throughout the year.

During colonization, the Algonquin became heavily involved in the fur trade. As the first tribe upriver from Montreal, they had a strategic market advantage as fur trade intermediaries. In addition to trading pelts they obtained directly from the hunt, the Algonquin traded maize and furs from tribes in the North American interior for French manufactured goods.

Algonquin descendants numbered more than 5,000 in the early 21st century.

CONOY

The Conoy (Piscataway) are related to the Delaware and the Nanticoke. Before colonization by the English, they lived between the Potomac River and the western shore of Chesapeake Bay in what is now Maryland. Early accounts suggest that their economy was based mainly on hunting the abundant game and fowl of the area, using bows and arrows and spears, and that they lived in oval-shaped dwellings.

Harassed by the Susquehannock (Susquehanna) in the 17th century, the rapidly decreasing Conoy retreated up the Potomac and into Pennsylvania. They gradually migrated up the Susquehanna River, and by 1765 the 150 members of the tribe, dependent on the Iroquois, had reached southern New York. They moved west with the Mohican and the Delaware, becoming part of these tribes.

DELAWARE

The Delaware (Lenni Lenape) call themselves Lenape. They are a confederation of peoples who occupied the Atlantic seaboard from Cape Henlopen, Delaware, to western Long Island. Before colonization, they were especially concentrated in the Delaware River valley, for which the confederation was named.

Traditionally, the Delaware depended primarily on agriculture, with hunting and fishing as important additions to their economy. Summer farming communities numbered several hundred persons. In winter, smaller family bands traveled throughout smaller territories to hunt. Delaware individuals were members of one of three clans, based on maternal descent. Clans were in turn divided into lineages, whose members generally lived together in a longhouse. Groups of longhouses formed the core of autonomous communities, of which there were probably 30 or 40 in 1600. A council consisting of lineage sachems (chiefs) and other distinguished men decided the public affairs of the community. The eldest woman of the lineage appointed and dismissed the sachem.

The Delaware were the Native Americans most friendly to William Penn. They were rewarded by the infamous Walking Purchase, a treaty that deprived them of their own lands and forced them to settle on lands assigned to the Iroquois. Encroached on by European colonizers and dominated by the Iroquois after 1690, they drifted westward in stages, stopping on the Susquehanna, the Allegheny, and the Muskingum rivers in Ohio and the White River in Indiana. After 60 years of displacement, Delaware individuals living beyond the Ohio River rekindled a tribal alliance, asserted their independence of the Iroquois, and opposed the advancing colonists. They defeated the British general Edward Braddock in the French and Indian War and at first supported the Americans in the revolution. In the Treaty of Greenville (1795) they ceded their Ohio lands. Many of the bands dispersed, but by 1835 some had gathered again in Kansas. Most of these were removed to Oklahoma in 1867. Delaware descendants numbered more than 16,900 in the early 21st century.

FOX

When they first met French traders in 1667, the tribe lived in the forest zone of what is now northeastern Wisconsin. Sometimes called Meskwaki, or Mesquakie, the Fox people called themselves Meshkwakihug, meaning the "Red-Earth People."

Traditionally, the Fox moved with the seasons. Their permanent villages—located near fields in which women cultivated maize (corn), beans, and squash—were occupied during the planting, growing, and harvest seasons. Most people left the villages after the harvest to participate in communal winter bison hunts on the prairies. Fox social and political organization was centred upon a peace chief and council of elders who administered tribal affairs. Important issues were discussed by the entire tribe until consensus was reached. War parties

Fox men in traditional clothing, photograph by C.M. Bell, c. 1890. Library of Congress, Washington, D.C. (neg. no. LC-USZ62-92960)

rallied about men whose skill and reputation made them leaders. Families were grouped into clans that were mainly ceremonial organizations. Members traced their descent from a mythical founder through the male line. A major religious organization was the Midewiwin, or Grand Medicine Society, a group whose members were devoted to healing the sick and enlisting supernatural aid to ensure tribal welfare. Many Midewiwin ceremonies involved the use of medicine bundles, which were collections of sacred objects.

In the 18th century the Fox joined with the Sauk (Sac) in resisting colonization by the French and later by the English. The two tribes eventually retreated from the colonial front by moving from what is now Wisconsin to Illinois and then Iowa. They moved to Kansas in 1842, and in 1857 some returned to Iowa.

Early 21st-century population estimates indicated more than 6,500 Fox descendants, most living in Iowa, Kansas, and Oklahoma.

ILLINOIS

A confederacy of small tribes—including the Cahokia, Kaskaskia, Michigamea, Peoria, and Tamaroa—were called the Illinois. Member tribes were spread over what are now southern Wisconsin and northern Illinois and parts of Missouri and Iowa.

Like other Northeast Indians, the Illinois traditionally lived in villages, their dwellings covered with rush mats and housing several families each. The Illinois economy combined agriculture with foraging. Women cultivated maize (corn) and other plant foods, small parties took forest mammals and wild plants throughout the year, and most members of a given village participated in one or more winter bison hunts on the prairie. Little is known of Illinois social organization, but it was probably similar to that of the Miami, with a civil chief elected from among a village council and a war chief chosen according to his ability to lead raids.

By the middle of the 17th century, most of the Illinois people were living along the Illinois River from Starved Rock to the Mississippi, having moved there because of harassment by the Dakota Sioux, Fox, and other northern tribes. Iroquois raids greatly reduced their numbers, and the introduction of liquor by French traders further weakened the tribe. The murder of the Ottawa chief Pontiac by an Illinois individual provoked the vengeance of several northern Algonquian tribes, further reducing the Illinois population. The survivors took refuge with French settlers in Kaskaskia, while the Sauk, Fox, Kickapoo, and Potawatomi took most of the remaining

Illinois territory. In 1832 the Illinois sold the lands they had retained, moving to Kansas and then to Indian Territory (present-day Oklahoma).

Early 21st-century population estimates indicated more than 1,500 individuals of Illinois descent.

KICKAPOO

The Kickapoo are related to the Sauk and Fox. When first reported by Europeans in the late 17th century, the Kickapoo lived at the portage between the Fox and Wisconsin rivers, probably in present-day Columbia county, Wisconsin. They were known as formidable warriors whose raids took them over a wide territory, ranging as far as Georgia and Alabama to the southeast, Texas and Mexico to the southwest, and New York and Pennsylvania to the east.

From the beginning of European contact, the Kickapoo resisted acculturation in economic, political, and religious matters, retaining as many of their old ways as possible. Traditionally, the Kickapoo lived in fixed villages, moving between summer and winter residences. They raised maize (corn), beans, and squash and hunted buffalo on the prairies. Their society was divided into several exogamous clans based on descent through the paternal line.

In the early 18th century part of the tribe settled near the Milwaukee River. After the destruction of the Illinois Indians about 1765, the Milwaukee River band moved south into the Illinois' former territory near Peoria, Ill. By the 19th century, as a result of scattering in small villages to prevent attack, central tribal authority had broken down, and the chiefs of the various bands had become autonomous. One group moved as far as the Sangamon River and became known as the Prairie band. Another pushed east to the Wabash and was called the Vermilion band. In 1809 and 1819, under the pressure of advancing American settlers, the Kickapoo ceded their lands in Illinois to the United States, moving to Missouri and then to Kansas. About 1852 a large group went to Texas and from there to Mexico, where they were joined by another party in 1863. Some returned to Indian Territory (present-day Oklahoma) in 1873 and later years. Those who stayed in Mexico were granted a reservation in eastern Chihuahua state.

In the early 21st century, Kickapoo descendants in the United States numbered more than 5,000, with about 300 in Mexico.

MALECITE

The Malecite (or Maliseet) occupied the Saint John valley in what is now New Brunswick, Can., and the northeastern corner of what is now the U.S. state of Maine. Their language was closely related to that of the Passamaquoddy, and they were members of the Abenaki Confederacy, a group of tribes mentioned previously that was organized for protection against the Iroquois Confederacy.

Traditionally, the Malecite practiced maize (corn) cultivation, as well as hunting and fishing. Birch bark, wood, stone, and ceramics were used for the manufacture of utensils, tools, and weapons. A tribal council consisting of a war chief, a civil chief, and representatives of each family decided most tribal questions. A general council of the entire tribe decided war matters on a consensus basis.

Although the Malecite were probably interacting with English and French explorers as early as the middle of the 16th century, the first record of such contact dates from Samuel de Champlain's voyage of 1604. Fort La Tour, built on the Saint John River early in the 17th century, became a centre for trade and cultural exchange. The few French settlers in that area intermarried with the tribe, strengthening the Malecite alliance with the French as well as the tribe's hostility to the English. The English gained control of eastern Canada following the French and Indian War, and the tribe disputed the new colonizer's land claims until 1776, after which certain lands were assigned to the tribe. By 1856 their territory had been reduced to the Tobique River valley and another small tract.

Population estimates indicated more than 2,000 individuals of Malecite descent in the early 21st century.

MASSACHUSET

In the 17th century, the Massachuset tribe may have numbered 3,000 individuals living in more than 20 villages

Puritan missionary John Eliot preaching to the Native Americans of the region around Massachusetts Bay Colony. His translation of the Bible into the Algonquian language was the first Bible printed in North America. MPI/Archive Photos/Getty Images

distributed along what is now the Massachusetts coast. They cultivated maize (corn) and other vegetables, gathered wild plants, and hunted and fished. The people moved seasonally between fixed sites to exploit different wild food resources as they became available. The tribe was divided into bands, each ruled by a chief, or sachem.

Even before colonial settlement began in the immediate area, the Massachuset population had been greatly reduced by warfare with their northeastern neighbours, the Tarratine. The tribe was decimated by a pestilence in 1617. A smallpox epidemic in 1633 wiped out most remaining members of the tribe, including the chief. Christian missionaries, notably John Eliot, gathered converts from the Massachuset and other tribes into new villages in which distinct tribal identities often merged. The state of Massachusetts is named for this tribe.

MENOMINEE

When first encountered by the missionary-voyageur Jean Nicolet in 1639, the Menominee (Menomini) lived along the Menominee River, now the eastern portion of the boundary between Wisconsin and the upper peninsula of Michigan.

The traditional Menominee economy was based, in order of importance, on gathering wild rice and other wild plants; cultivating maize (corn), squash, beans, and tobacco; and fishing and hunting. Before colonization the people lived in permanent villages of dome-shaped houses. Menominee people reckoned kinship through clan membership, and individuals from the same clan were not allowed to marry. The clans, in turn, belonged to one of two major divisions, or moieties, within the tribe. After the advent of the fur trade the Menominee spent increasing amounts of time dispersed in mobile bands over a wide territory, particularly for winter hunts.

In 19th-century treaties the Menominee ceded land to the U.S. government yet retained the permanent right to use their former territory for hunting, fishing, and other subsistence activities. In 1852 some 2,000 members of the tribe were removed to a reservation on the upper Wolf and Oconto rivers in Wisconsin. Beginning in 1872, a tribally owned lumber mill operated under government supervision, providing the community with jobs and income. In the early 21st century the tribe remained heavily invested in the mill and was an innovator in the sustainable production of lumber.

In the mid-20th century the U.S. government instituted a movement known as termination, in which tribes lost federal recognition and the benefits and protections associated with that status. The Menominee reservation was terminated in 1961. The former reservation lands became a county within the state of Wisconsin, and a corporation, Menominee Enterprises, Inc., was created to hold and administer tribal assets. Soon after termination many tribal members became concerned about the loss of services and self-determination that had been ensured by reservation status. Issues of particular concern included the elimination of subsidized health care, which left the community with no hospital and no resident physician, and the sale of former reservation lands to non-Indians. The Menominee began agitating for the restoration of federal status, which was granted by the U.S. Congress in December 1973.

Population estimates indicated more than 9,500 individuals of Menominee descent in the early 21st century.

MIAMI

The Miami lived in the area of what is now Green Bay, Wis., when first encountered by French explorers in the

17th century. The Miami also lived in established settlements at the southern end of Lake Michigan in what are now northeastern Illinois and northern Indiana and on the Kalamazoo River in what is now Michigan. They continued to expand as far as Detroit and Ohio but later withdrew from their eastern territories and settled in Indiana.

Miami social organization was based on exogamous, or out-marrying, clans. Because it mandates marriage between, rather than within, extended family groups, this form of kinship fostered strongly interconnected communities. Clan chiefs served as members of the village council. One of their number was elected civil chief. A separate war chief was chosen on the basis of ability in leading raids. At the time of the first French contact, the Miami were divided into six bands, of which two, the Wea and the Piankashaw, later became separate tribes.

The staple of the traditional Miami diet was a particular type of maize (corn) that they considered superior to that cultivated by their neighbours. During the summer the Miami occupied permanent agricultural villages. In the winter they moved to the prairies for communal bison hunts. In addition to mat-covered dwellings, each village had a large building in which councils and ceremonies were held. A major feature of Miami religion was the Midewiwin, or Grand Medicine Society, a religious organization whose members were believed to be able to cure the sick and secure supernatural aid for tribal welfare. Sacred medicine bundles of magical objects were important in many Miami rites and ceremonies.

In the 19th century the Miami ceded most of their lands to the United States, and many moved to a reservation in Indian Territory (Oklahoma) in 1867.

Population estimates indicated approximately 6,500 Miami descendants in the early 21st century.

MI'KMAQ

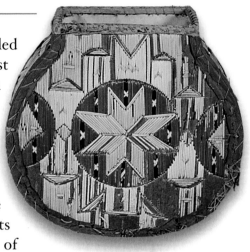

The Mi'kmaq (also spelled Micmac) were the largest North American Indian tribe who tradition- ally occupied what are now Canada's eastern Maritime Provinces (Nova Scotia, New Brunswick, and Prince Edward Island) and parts of the present states of Maine and Massachusetts. Because their Algonquian dialect differed greatly from that of their neigh- bours, it is thought that the Mi'kmaq settled the area later than other tribes in the region.

Mi'kmaq bark box embroidered with porcupine quills; in the Denver Art Museum. Courtesy of the Denver Art Museum, Colorado

Historically, the Mi'kmaq were probably the tribe that Italian explorer John Cabot first encountered in 1497. Although early European chroniclers described them as fierce and warlike, they were among the first native peoples to accept Jesuit teachings and to inter- marry with the settlers of New France. In the 17th and 18th centuries the Mi'kmaq were allies of the French against the English, frequently traveling south to raid the New England frontiers.

Traditionally, the Mi'kmaq were seasonally nomadic. In winter they hunted caribou, moose, and small game. In summer they fished and gathered shellfish and hunted seals on the coasts. Winter dwellings were conical wickiups (wigwams) covered with birch bark or skins.

Summer dwellings were varied, usually oblong wigwams, relatively open-air. Mi'kmaq clothing was similar to that of other Northeast Indians. Both men and women wore robes made of fur (later of blankets), while men typically wore loincloths and women dresses. Clothing was generally ornamented with ample amounts of fringe.

Mi'kmaq social and political life was flexible and loosely organized, with an emphasis on kin relations. They were part of the Abenaki Confederacy, a group of Algonquian-speaking tribes allied in mutual hostility against the Iroquois Confederacy.

Population estimates indicated some 14,000 Mi'kmaq descendants in the early 21st century.

MOHEGAN

Originally the Mohegan occupied land in what is now Connecticut, covering most of the upper Thames valley. Fighting with other tribes also led to the seizure of land in Massachusetts and Rhode Island. The Mohegan are not to be confused with the Mohican (Mahican), who originally resided in the upper Hudson River valley near the Catskill Mountains in what is now New York state.

The traditional Mohegan economy was based on the cultivation of maize (corn) and on hunting and fishing. At the time of the first European settlement of New England early in the 17th century, the Mohegan and the Pequot tribes were ruled jointly by the Pequot chief, Sassacus. Later a rebellion by the subchief Uncas led to Mohegan independence. After the destruction of the Pequot in 1637, most of the Pequot survivors and the former Pequot territories came under Mohegan control. Uncas strengthened his position by making an alliance with the English. By the end of King Philip's War against the colonists, the Mohegan were the strongest tribe remaining in southern New England. Colonial settlements gradually displaced the Mohegan, and their numbers dwindled from imported diseases and other hardships. Many of them joined other native settlements.

Population estimates indicated some 2,500 Mohegan descendants in the early 21st century.

MOHICAN

The Mohican (Mahican) lived in what is now the upper Hudson River valley above the Catskill Mountains in New York state. Their name for themselves, Muh-he-con-neok, means "the people of the waters that are never still." During the colonial period, they were known to the Dutch and the English as the River Indians and to the French as the Loups ("Wolves"). The Mohican are not to be confused with the Mohegan, who originally resided in what is now Connecticut and are related to the Pequot.

Before colonization, the Mohican consisted of at least five bands and were further organized by three matrilineal clans. The latter were governed by hereditary sachems, or chiefs, who were assisted by elected counselors. Tribal members lived in strongholds of 20 to 30 houses, situated on hills and enclosed by stockades, as well as in enclosed villages situated between maize (corn) fields and woodland.

When first contacted by the Dutch, the Mohican were at war with the Mohawk, and in 1664 they were forced to move from Schodack, near Albany, to what is now Stockbridge, Mass. They gradually sold their territory there, and in 1736 some of them were gathered into a mission at Stockbridge and became known as the Stockbridge band. Other groups scattered and merged with other tribes. The Stockbridge band later moved to Wisconsin and were joined by the Munsee band. The two groups were allotted a joint reservation in Wisconsin in the 19th century. The American novelist James Fenimore Cooper drew a romanticized portrait of the Mohican in his book *The Last of the Mohicans* (1826).

Population estimates indicated approximately 3,500 Mohican descendants in the early 21st century.

MONTAUK

The name Montauk refers to both a single tribe and a confederacy of tribes who lived on the eastern and central parts of what is now Long Island, N.Y. The confederacy included the Shinnecock, Manhasset, Massapequa, Montauk proper, Patchogue, and Rockaway tribes. Like other Algonquian tribes of this area, the Montauk proper depended for their subsistence largely on women's cultivation of maize (corn), which was supplemented by men's hunting and community-wide fishing. They were semisedentary, moving seasonally between fixed sites as food resources required.

The Montauk proper were dominated by the Pequot until the destruction of that tribe in 1637, after which the Narraganset attacked the tribe and its allies. Disease further reduced the Montauk population, and in about 1659 the estimated 500 remaining members of the tribe sought refuge with English colonists at Easthampton. By 1788 only some 162 Montauk tribal members remained.

Population estimates indicated some 700 Montauk descendants in the early 21st century.

NARRAGANSET

The tribe that originally occupied most of what is now the U.S. state of Rhode Island west of the bay named for them was the Narraganset. They had eight divisions, each with a territorial chief who was in turn subject to a head chief. Their subsistence depended on the cultivation of maize (corn), hunting, and fishing.

The Narraganset maintained good relations with English colonizers until King Philip's War in 1675–76, in which they joined with other tribes in attempting to limit colonial expansion. In 1675, soon after a battle in which nearly 1,000 members of the tribe were killed or captured, the Narraganset abandoned their territory. Most joined the Mohican or Abenaki tribes or fled to Canada, from where some later received permission to return. Many of the latter settled in New York state among Algonquian groups that had remained neutral in the war, others joined the Mohegan in Connecticut, and a few moved to what is now Rhode Island.

Early 21st-century population estimates indicated some 4,500 individuals of Narraganset descent.

NAUSET

Also called Cape Indians, the Nauset occupied most of what is now Cape Cod, in Massachusetts. They probably came into contact with Europeans at an early date because of their location, and Samuel de Champlain is known to have encountered them in 1606. Their subsistence was probably based on fishing, hunting, and gathering wild foods. They are also known to have cultivated maize (corn), beans, and squash. They were semisedentary, moving between fixed sites in order to take advantage of seasonal changes in food resources.

Although hostile to the Plymouth colonists at first, the Nauset later became their friends, supplying food to the starving colonists in 1622. Most Nauset remained loyal to the British settlers throughout King Philip's War. Many converted to Christianity before the war, and by 1710 all were organized into churches. In that year many died of fever, and by 1802 only four Nauset were said to survive. However, the Nauset and other tribes, principally the Wampanoag, had intermarried after being driven from their original territories. Their descendants numbered more than 4,500 in the early 21st century.

NIANTIC

The Niantic were woodland Indians of southern New England. The Eastern Niantic lived on the western coast of what is now Rhode Island and on the neighbouring coast of Connecticut. The Western Niantic lived on the seacoast from Niantic Bay, just west of New London, to the Connecticut River. Once one tribe, they were apparently split by the migration of the Pequot into their area.

The Western Niantic were nearly destroyed by the Pequot War (1637), and remnants joined the Mohegan. The Eastern Niantic remained neutral during King Philip's War (1675–76), and at its close many of the defeated Narraganset Indians and their allies settled among the Niantic. Thereafter the combined tribes were called Narraganset.

NIPMUC

The Nipmuc originally occupied the central plateau of what is now the state of Massachusetts and extended into what are now northern Rhode Island and Connecticut. Their subsistence was based on hunting, fishing, and the cultivation of maize (corn). They moved seasonally between fixed sites to exploit these food resources. The Nipmuc were divided into territorial bands, or groups of related families living in one or more villages. Each village was ruled by a sachem, or chief. The many Nipmuc villages were not united politically. Rather than forming a pan-Nipmuc alliance, each village allied with its more powerful neighbours, such as the Massachuset, Wampanoag, Narraganset, and Mohegan.

By 1674 New England missionaries had established seven villages of Christian converts, but in the following year most of the Nipmuc joined King Philip and other hostile tribes in an attempt to force the colonists to leave New England. At the close of the war they fled to Canada or to the Mohican and other tribes on the Hudson River.

Early 21st-century population estimates indicated approximately 1,500 individuals of Nipmuc descent.

OJIBWA

The Ojibwa (Ojibwe, or Ojibway) are also called Chippewa, but they call themselves Anishinaabe. They lived in what are now Ontario and Manitoba, Can., and Minnesota and North Dakota, U.S., from Lake Huron westward onto the Plains. Their name for themselves means "original people." In Canada those Ojibwa who lived west of Lake Winnipeg are called the Saulteaux. When first reported in the *Relations* of 1640, an annual report by the Jesuit missionaries in New France, the Ojibwa occupied a comparatively restricted region near the St. Mary's River and in the Upper Peninsula of the present state of Michigan. They moved west as the fur trade expanded, in response to pressure from tribes to their east and new opportunities to their west.

Traditionally, each Ojibwa tribe was divided into migratory bands. In the autumn, bands separated into family units, which dispersed to individual hunting areas. In summer, families gathered together, usually at fishing sites. The Ojibwa relied on the collection of wild rice for a major part of their diet, and a few bands also cultivated maize (corn). Birch bark was used extensively for canoes, dome-shaped wigwams, and utensils. Clan intermarriage served to connect a people that otherwise avoided overall tribal or national chiefs. Chieftainship of a band was not a powerful office until dealings with fur traders strengthened the position, which then became hereditary through the paternal line. The major Ojibwa ceremonial was an annual celebration hosted by the Midewiwin (Grand Medicine Society), a secret religious organization open to men and women. Membership was believed to provide supernatural assistance and conferred prestige on its members.

The Ojibwa constituted one of the largest indigenous North American groups in the early 21st century, when population estimates indicated some 175,000 individuals of Ojibwa descent.

OTTAWA

The original territory of the Ottawa focused on the Ottawa River, the French River, and Georgian Bay, in present northern Michigan, U.S., and southeastern Ontario and southwestern Quebec, Can. According to tradition, the Ottawa, Ojibwa, and Potawatomi were formerly one tribe, having migrated from the northwest and separated at what is now Mackinaw, Mich. The earliest known location of the Ottawa was on Manitoulin Island.

The Ottawa were widely known as traders. Their location and negotiating skills enabled them to become middlemen in intertribal commerce. Their canoes traveled as far west as Green Bay, Wis., and as far east as Quebec to buy and sell such merchandise as cornmeal, furs, sunflower oil, mats, tobacco, and medicinal herbs. Before colonization by the French and English, the

Ottawa were semisedentary, living in agricultural villages in summer and separating into family groups for winter hunts. Planting and harvesting crops were women's occupations. Hunting and fishing were the responsibility of men. Ottawa villages were sometimes palisaded for protection.

In the late 17th century the tribe comprised four, or possibly five, major divisions, which were subdivided into local bands. They are believed to have had several clans distributed among the bands. Attacked by the Iroquois, the Ottawa fled, some joining the Potawatomi at Green Bay, others dispersing throughout the Lower Peninsula of Michigan, Wisconsin, and northern Illinois.

Early 21st-century population estimates indicated some 14,000 individuals of Ottawa descent.

PAMLICO

The Pamlico lived along the Pamlico River in what is now Beaufort county, N.C., when first encountered by Europeans. These sedentary agriculturists were almost destroyed by smallpox in 1696, and in 1710 the 75 survivors lived in a single village. They joined with part of the Tuscarora and other tribes in a war against white settlers (1711–13). At the close of the war those Tuscarora under treaty with the English agreed to exterminate the Pamlico. The surviving remnant were probably incorporated as slaves to the Tuscarora.

PASSAMAQUODDY

The Passamaquoddy lived on Passamaquoddy Bay, the St. Croix River, and Schoodic Lake on the boundary between what are now Maine, U.S., and New Brunswick, Can.

At the time of European contact, the Passamaquoddy belonged to the Abenaki Confederacy, and their language was closely related to that of the Malecite. They traditionally depended on hunting and fishing for subsistence. Birch bark and wood were used for manufacture. Villages, consisting of conical dwellings and a large council house, were sometimes palisaded. A tribal council of the war chief, the civil chief, and representatives of each family decided most important matters. A general council of the entire tribe decided war matters. Over time colonial settlement encroached upon Passamaquoddy territory, and by 1866 the tribe had coalesced mainly at Sipayik (Sebaik), on the south side of Passamaquoddy Bay, and on Lewis Island.

Early 21st-century population estimates indicated approximately 6,000 individuals of Passamaquoddy descent.

PENNACOOK

The Pennacook lived in what are now southern and central New Hampshire, northeastern Massachusetts, and southern Maine. Their economy depended on hunting, fishing, and the cultivation of maize (corn). They were semisedentary, moving seasonally in response to the availability of food resources.

Smallpox and other causes reduced the Pennacook population from an estimated 2,000 in 1600 to 1,250 in 1674. The treachery of European colonists subsequently caused the Pennacook to flee their territory, most removing to Canada and eventually settling at Saint-François-du-Lac. The remainder moved westward and eventually settled at Schaghticoke, Rensselaer county, N.Y.

PENOBSCOT

Penobscot Bay and the Penobscot River basin in what is now the state of Maine was home to the Penobscot people. They were members of the Abenaki Confederacy. Penobscot subsistence was based on hunting, fishing, and collecting wild plants, with seasonal movement to obtain food. In winter small family groups lived in hunting camps within separate family territories, rights to which were inherited through the male line. Larger camps and villages were inhabited during the summer. The tribal chief embodied little power, generally acting as a tribal representative in ceremonies or in dealings with outsiders and sometimes adjudicating disputes.

Europeans first encountered the Penobscot early in the 16th century. A French mission was established among them in 1688. The Penobscot assisted the French against the English in all the wars on the New England frontier until 1749, when they made peace with the English. As a result, they did not move to Canada with the other groups of the Abenaki Confederacy, and they remain in their old territory to the present. The Penobscot and the Passamaquoddy send a nonvoting representative to Maine's state legislature.

Early 21st-century population estimates indicated some 4,000 Penobscot descendants.

PEQUOT

The Pequot inhabited the Thames valley in what is now Connecticut. Their subsistence was based on the cultivation of maize (corn), hunting, and fishing. In the 1600s their population was estimated to be 2,200 individuals.

The Mohegan and the Pequot were jointly ruled by the Pequot chief Sassacus until a rebellion of the subchief Uncas resulted in Mohegan independence. For a period from 1620 onward the Pequot and British settlers lived side by side in mutual helpfulness and peaceful trade. Gradually, however, Pequot resentment swelled as increasing numbers of colonists encroached upon the tribe's customary territory. The Pequot were concerned regarding these intrusions because their territory had already been reduced to the region between Narragansett Bay and the Connecticut River. The Pequot eventually promised all tribal trade to the Dutch, a course of action much resented by the British.

Several incidents had taken place between the Pequot and the British colonizers by the summer of 1636, when matters came to a breaking point. At that time a Boston trader was murdered, presumably by a Pequot, on Block Island. A punitive expedition that was sent by Massachusetts authorities to destroy native villages and crops succeeded only in arousing the tribe to make a more determined defense of its homeland. Puritan clergymen encouraged violence against the Pequot, whom they regarded as infidels, and the British colonists agreed to take up arms.

In a short but vicious war, in which Captain John Mason led English, Mohegan, and Narraganset warriors, the main Pequot fort at Mystic, Conn., was surprised and set afire. Between 500 and 600 inhabitants were burned alive or slaughtered. Defeated, some Pequot decided to separate into small bands and abandon the area. Many who fled were killed or captured by other tribes or the English, and others were sold into slavery in New England or the West Indies. The remainder were distributed among other tribes, where they received such harsh treatment that in 1655 they were placed under the direct control of the colonial government and resettled on the Mystic River. The Mohegan obtained control of Pequot lands.

Early 21st-century population estimates indicated approximately 3,000 Pequot descendants.

POCOMTUC

The Pocomtuc lived in what is now western Massachusetts and adjoining parts of Connecticut and Vermont in the United States. In 1600 they were estimated to number 1,200. Like other New England tribes they were semi-sedentary, moving seasonally between relatively permanent sites. Their main diet was maize (corn), cultivated by the Pocomtuc women, and fish and game.

In 1675 the Pocomtuc joined in King Philip's War against the colonists and, after the war, fled to Scaticook, along the Hudson River. Some remained there until 1754, when they joined other Indian tribes at Saint-François-du-Lac, Canada.

POWHATAN

The Powhatan constituted a confederacy of at least 30 tribes that once occupied most of what is now tidewater Virginia, the eastern shore of the Chesapeake Bay, and possibly southern Maryland. The confederacy had been formed by and named for a powerful chief, Powhatan, shortly before the colonial settlement of Jamestown in 1607. The tribes of the confederacy provided mutual military support and paid taxes to Powhatan in the form of food, pelts, copper, and pearls. Many of the confederacy's villages, which consisted of long dwellings covered with bark or reed mats, were palisaded. They were situated near fields in which women cultivated maize (corn), beans, squash, and other vegetables. Men were occupied with hunting and warfare.

A colourized engraving of Pocahontas, daughter of Chief Powhatan (seated, left) stopping the execution of Englishman John Smith. Skirmishes between the Powhatan and British settlers were frequent. Kean Collection/ Archive Photos/Getty Images

Hostilities developed between the Powhatan Confederacy and the English settlers and resulted in intermittent fighting until 1676. Long-standing conflicts with the Iroquois were ended by a treaty in 1722, but the greatly reduced Powhatan population continued to decline. Those on the eastern shore of Virginia, who had long intermarried with free and enslaved Africans, were driven off in 1831 during the disturbances caused by a slave rebellion led by Nat Turner.

In the early 21st century population estimates indicated approximately 2,000 individuals of Powhatan descent.

SAUK

When first encountered by the French in 1667, the Sauk (Sac) lived in the region of what is now Green Bay, Wis. They are closely related to other Algonquian-speaking tribes, notably the Fox and the Kickapoo.

The Sauk made encampments and subsisted in groupings that were partly dictated by the seasons. In the summer, they lived in permanent bark-house villages near fields filled with maize (corn) and other crops. After the harvest the village separated into family groups that erected winter houses, which consisted of poles covered with reed mats. In spring the tribe gathered on the Iowa prairies to hunt bison.

Patrilineal clans regulated the inheritance of personal names and controlled certain religious ceremonies. Other ceremonies were sponsored by secret societies, such as the Midewiwin, or Grand Medicine Society, whose members were believed to be able to heal the sick and to enlist supernatural aid for the tribe. Many rituals involved the use of sacred medicine bundles, which were collections of holy objects. The Sauk were governed by a tribal council and hereditary chiefs. When war broke out, these were temporarily replaced by war chiefs selected for their military ability.

By the 19th century the Sauk had settled along the Mississippi River between what are now Rock Island, Ill., and St. Louis, Mo. In 1804 some of their minor chiefs ceded most of the tribal lands to the United States. Although the Sauk protested that this treaty was illegal, they were unable to prevent its enforcement. The resulting unrest

Tah-Col-O-Quoit (Rising Cloud), a Sauk Warrior, *lithograph by J.T. Brown, c. 1842.* Library of Congress, Washington, D.C.

led to the Black Hawk War (1832), after which the Sauk were forced to relinquish more territory. They moved to Iowa, then Kansas, and finally settled in Indian Territory (Oklahoma) at the end of the 19th century.

Early 21st-century population estimates indicated some 7,000 individuals of Sauk descent.

SHAWNEE

The Shawnee lived in what is now the central Ohio River valley. Closely related in language and culture to the Fox, Kickapoo, and Sauk, the Shawnee were also influenced by a long association with the Seneca and Delaware.

During the summer the Shawnee lived in bark-covered houses. Their large villages were located near the fields in which women cultivated maize (corn) and other vegetables. The primary male occupation was hunting. In winter village residents dispersed to family hunting camps. Each village had a large council house that was also used for such religious ceremonies as the ritual purification of warriors. Other important ceremonies included the spring Bread Dance, held when the fields were planted; the Green Corn Dance, marking the ripening of crops; and the autumn Bread Dance. The Shawnee comprised five major divisions, each further organized through a number of patrilineal clans. The position of civil chief was generally hereditary, while war chiefs were chosen for their bravery, skill, and experience.

In the 17th century the Shawnee were driven from their home by the Iroquois, scattering into widely separated areas. Some settled in what is now Illinois and others in the Cumberland Valley, while one group moved to the southeast. After 1725 the tribe reunited in Ohio, where they formed the principal barrier to the advance of colonial settlers.

TECUMSEH AND THE PROPHET

The great Shawnee chief Tecumseh (1768–1813) and his brother Tenskwatawa (1775–1834), a religious leader known as the Prophet, together led one of the most dramatic Indian struggles to resist the encroachment of Euro-Americans into the Northwest Territory (a parcel of land established by Congress in 1787 and from which the states of Ohio, Indiana, Illinois, Michigan, and Wisconsin were ultimately organized). From earliest childhood the brothers had witnessed the suffering of the Shawnee at the hands of white settlers, and together they undertook the establishment of a pan-tribal confederacy.

In 1805 the Prophet declared that he had a message from the Master of Life, who would reward the Shawnee if they returned to distinctively indigenous ways of life and rejected colonial customs such as the use of alcohol, clothing made of textiles rather than animal skins and furs, the concept of individual ownership of property, and intermarriage with those of European descent. The Prophet engaged his followers by describing the supernatural contacts he instigated through incantations and dreams. He won credibility when he accurately predicted a solar eclipse in 1806.

In 1808 Tecumseh and Tenskwatawa established a village that came to be known as Prophet's Town near the site of present-day Battle Ground in northern Indiana. They persuaded those who joined them at Prophet's Town to follow the traditional way of life advocated by the Prophet.

Meanwhile Tecumseh was forming a defensive tribal confederacy, traveling throughout the East and Midwest. "Our fathers," he said to the people he met with, "from their tombs, reproach us as slaves and cowards." With such powerful words, he won the allegiance of many tribes.

At that time William Henry Harrison (who would become the ninth president of the United States) was governor of the Indiana Territory. In this role, he induced a number of individual tribes to give up great parcels of land in the region that is now Indiana and Illinois. At a council held in Vincennes in 1810, Tecumseh demanded that land be returned. Because it belonged to all of them, he argued, and was not the property of one group, individual chiefs did not have the right to barter it away. His demand was rejected. He then traveled to Canada to consult the British and afterward to the Southwest to enlist support of Indian tribes there.

In September 1811, during Tecumseh's absence, Harrison undertook an expedition against Prophet's Town. The Prophet, who was not a warrior like his brother, allowed the Shawnee to be drawn into military action, and told his men that the white man's bullets would not harm them. On November 7, after the fiercely fought Battle of Tippecanoe, Harrison and his men utterly destroyed the village. This defeat thoroughly discredited the Prophet, who fled to Canada, and scattered the Indian warriors. The event destroyed the pan-tribal confederacy that Tecumseh and the Prophet had worked so hard to achieve and effectively extinguished Indian resistance in the Midwest. When the War of 1812 broke out, Tecumseh joined the British as a brigadier general. He was killed at the Battle of the Thames and is buried on Walpole Island, Ont. The Prophet later resettled with other Indians on a reservation in Kansas.

Following their defeat by Gen. Anthony Wayne at the Battle of Fallen Timbers (1794) and the failure of Tecumseh's alliance to prevent further colonial encroachment in the Ohio Valley, the Shawnee broke into three independent branches, the Absentee, Eastern, and Cherokee Shawnee, that eventually settled in different parts of Oklahoma.

Early 21st-century population estimates indicated some 12,000 individuals of Shawnee descent.

WAMPANOAG

Traditionally a semisedentary people, the Wampanoag moved seasonally between fixed sites. They formerly occupied parts of what are now the states of Rhode Island and Massachusetts, including Martha's Vineyard, Nantucket, and adjacent islands. The tribe comprised several villages, each with its own local chief, or sachem. Maize (corn) was the staple of their diet, supplemented by fish and game.

In 1620 the Wampanoag high chief, Massasoit, made a peace treaty with the Pilgrims, who had landed in the tribe's territory. The treaty was observed until Massasoit's death. Poor treatment by settlers who encroached on tribal lands, however, led his son, Metacom, or Metacomet, known to the English as King Philip, to organize a confederacy of tribes to drive out the colonists.

When the colonists eventually defeated and killed King Philip and other leading chiefs, the Wampanoag (along with another Northeastern tribe, the Narraganset) were almost exterminated. Some survivors fled to the interior, while others moved to the islands of Nantucket and Martha's Vineyard to join kin who had remained neutral during the conflict. Disease and epidemics destroyed

KING PHILIP'S WAR

The bloodiest conflict in 17th-century New England was King Philip's War, fought in 1675–76 between English settlers and Native Americans. Although it temporarily devastated the frontier communities, it eventually eradicated native military resistance to the European colonization of that region.

For years, mutual helpfulness and trade had been fostered by both the early Massachusetts colonists and the Indian leader Massasoit, grand sachem of the Wampanoag. The peace was first shattered by the Pequot War in 1637. By the 1660s settlers had outgrown their dependence on the Indians for wilderness survival techniques and had substituted fishing and commerce for the earlier lucrative fur trade. From 1640 to 1675 new waves of land-hungry settlers pushed into Indian territory, particularly in Massachusetts, Connecticut, and Rhode Island. Tribes had to fight to protect their homelands. Otherwise they would become "white men's vassals," subject to alien law, humiliating limitations on personal freedom, usurpation of favourite hunting grounds, and regulation by a strict Christian morality.

Upon Massasoit's death (1661) his successor and second son, Metacom (called King Philip by the settlers), vowed to resist further English expansion and attempted to organize a federation of tribes. Eventually Metacom won support from the powerful Narraganset and almost all of the other New England tribes. When three Wampanoag were executed (June 1675) for the murder of an informer, John Sassamon, Metacom could no longer hold his young warriors in check, and bloodshed erupted before either side could coordinate campaign plans. The war actually resolved itself into a series of ruthless Indian raids on frontier settlements from the Connecticut River to Massachusetts and Narragansett Bay, followed by brutal retaliatory assaults on Indian villages by the colonial militia. By the end of 1675 many frontier towns had been devastated, and the Narraganset had been wiped out in what was called the Great Swamp Fight. The Indians maintained a distinct advantage in the fighting until the spring of 1676, when their efforts were undermined by the threat of starvation after the destruction of their crops and when the English finally agreed to use "Praying Indians" (those who had converted to Christianity) as scouts. Following Metacom's death in August, Indian resistance collapsed, although Articles of Peace were not signed for two years.

King Philip's War was one of the costliest confrontations in colonial history: Edward Randolph, an agent of the crown, estimated that some 600 Europeans and 3,000 Indians lost their lives. It is believed that more than half of the 90 settlements in the region had been attacked and a dozen destroyed. Whole Indian villages were massacred and entire tribes decimated. Indigenous refugees fled westward and northward. Thereafter settlers felt free to expand without fear into former Indian territory across southern New England.

most of the indigenous people who lived on Nantucket, but Wampanoag people survive to the present, particularly on Martha's Vineyard.

Early 21st-century population estimates indicated some 4,500 Wampanoag descendants.

WAPPINGER

The Wappinger people were a confederacy of Indians in eastern North America. Early in the 17th century they lived along the east bank of the Hudson River from Manhattan Island to what is now Poughkeepsie and eastward to the lower Connecticut River valley.

Traditionally, the Wappinger were semisedentary, moving seasonally between fixed sites as food resources required. They depended largely on maize (corn), cultivated by women, for their subsistence. This was supplemented by hunting, fishing, and collecting wild plant foods. The tribes were divided into bands, each governed by a sachem (chief) and a council of elders.

Pressure from Dutch settlers caused the Connecticut Wappinger to sell their lands and join other Algonquian-speaking tribes elsewhere in what are today the United States and Canada. The western bands refused to do so. They fought the Dutch between 1640 and 1645, suffering severe losses. In 1756 the majority of the Wappinger remaining in Westchester county joined the Nanticoke at Chenango, N.Y., and then merged with the Delaware. Others joined the Stockbridge-Munsee tribe.

I roquoian languages were aboriginally spoken around the eastern Great Lakes and in parts of the Middle Atlantic states and the South. Aside from the languages of the Iroquois Confederacy (Mohawk, Oneida, Onondaga, Cayuga, and Seneca, all originally spoken in New York, along with Tuscarora, originally spoken in North Carolina) and Cherokee (originally spoken in the southern Appalachians), the Iroquoian languages are extinct, and the extinct languages are poorly documented (with the exception of Huron and Wyandot). Iroquoian languages are remarkable for their grammatical intricacy. Much of a sentence's semantic content is bound around a verbal base, so a single extremely long word may constitute a fairly complex utterance.

CAYUGA

The Cayuga originally inhabited the region bordering Cayuga Lake in what is now central New York state. Traditionally, Cayuga men hunted the abundant game, waterfowl, and fish of the region, and Cayuga women cultivated maize (corn). Villages consisted of multiple-fireside longhouses that sheltered related families. When first visited by the French Jesuit René Ménard in 1656, their towns occupied the lands east of the lake above the marshes south of the Seneca River. Approximately 1,500 people lived in some 100 longhouses. The local Cayuga council, which guided the village chiefs, comprised representatives of the eight exogamous clans. The clans were grouped into two major divisions, or moieties, which had largely ceremonial functions at funerals and games.

Historically, the Cayuga often allowed other groups to join their communities. When living in a refuge settlement north of Lake Ontario, they took in Huron and Erie captives to replace war losses, and in the late 17th century they provided refuge for many Siouan-speaking and Algonquian-speaking bands from the near south and west. At the beginning of the American revolution a large part of the Cayuga tribe, which favoured the British, moved to Canada. After the Revolution, the Cayuga remaining in the United States sold their New York lands and scattered among other Iroquois peoples in Wisconsin, Ohio, and Ontario. Cayuga descendants numbered more than 3,500 in the early 21st century.

ERIE

The Erie inhabited most of what is now northern Ohio, parts of northwestern Pennsylvania, and western New York. The name Erie is a truncation of Erielhonan (literally "Long Tail," and a reference to the panther, mountain lion, or cougar). Thus, they were often referred to as the Nation du chat (or "Cat Nation"). Little is known of their social or political organization, but early Jesuit accounts record that the Erie had many permanent, stockaded towns, practiced agriculture, and comprised several divisions. Erie traditions told of numerous wars with tribes of the Iroquois Confederacy. The final conflict occurred between 1653 and 1656, with the Erie being forced to capitulate when their bows and poisoned arrows were unable to withstand the guns supplied to the Iroquois by Dutch and English traders. Some of the surviving Erie fled to other tribes, but most were captured by the Iroquois and adopted as a constituent tribe.

HURON

The Huron were also called Wyandot or Wyandotte. They were living along the St. Lawrence River when contacted by French explorer Jacques Cartier in 1534. Many aspects of Huron culture were similar to those of other Northeast Indians. Traditionally, the Huron lived in villages of large bark-covered longhouses, each of which housed a matrilineal extended family. Some villages were protected by an encircling palisade. Agriculture was the mainstay of the Huron economy. Men cleared fields and women planted, tended, and harvested crops including maize (corn), beans, squash, and sunflowers. Hunting and fishing supplemented the diet.

The Huron were divided into matrilineal exogamous clans, each headed by a clan chief. All the clan chiefs of a village formed a council, which, with the village chief, decided civil affairs. Villages were grouped into bands (each of which had a band chief and a band council, consisting of village chiefs, to deal with civil matters affecting the entire band), and all the bands together constituted the Huron nation. A large council of band chiefs and their local councils dealt with matters concerning the whole tribe. Women were influential in Huron affairs, as each clan's senior women were responsible for selecting its political leaders.

The Huron were bitter enemies of tribes of the Iroquois Confederacy, with whom they competed in the fur trade. Before the 17th century the Iroquois drove some Huron from the St. Lawrence River westward into what is now Ontario, where related groups seem to have already

An engraving depicting Champlain (centre, with gun) *and Huron warriors fighting the Iroquois in the 17th century. The Huron were bitter enemies of the Iroquois Confederacy.* MPI/Archive Photos/Getty Images

been resident. Four of these bands (the Rock, Cord, Bear, and Deer peoples) formed a confederacy called the Wendat that was destroyed by Iroquois invasions in 1648–50. The survivors were either captured and forced to settle among their conquerors or driven west and north. The latter remnants drifted back and forth between Michigan, Wisconsin, Ontario, Ohio, and Quebec. During the French and Indian War in the mid-18th century, the Huron allied with the French against the British and the Iroquois Confederacy.

The Huron gradually reestablished some influence in Ohio and Michigan, but the U.S. government eventually forced tribal members to sell their lands. They subsequently migrated to Kansas and then to Indian Territory (present Oklahoma).

Early 21st-century population estimates indicated some 4,000 individuals of Huron descent.

IROQUOIS

The name Iroquois is a French derivation of Irinakhoiw, meaning "rattlesnakes"—a pejorative name given to them by their Algonquian enemies. The Iroquoian linguistic groups occupied a continuous territory around Lakes Ontario, Huron, and Erie, in present-day New York state and Pennsylvania (U.S.) and southern Ontario and Quebec (Canada). The tribe should not be confused with the Iroquois Confederacy, as the latter comprised a subset of five, and later six, tribes from within the broader language family.

As was typical of Northeast Indians before colonization, the Iroquois were semisedentary agriculturists who palisaded their villages in time of need. Each village typically comprised several hundred people. The Iroquois call themselves Hodenosaunee, meaning "people of the longhouse." They lived in large longhouses made of saplings and sheathed with elm bark, each housing many families. The longhouse family was the basic unit of traditional Iroquois society, which used a nested form of social organization: households (each representing a lineage) were divisions of clans, several clans constituted each moiety, and the two moieties combined to create a tribe.

Groups of men built houses and palisades, fished, hunted, and engaged in military activities. Groups of women produced crops of maize (corn), beans, and squash, gathered wild foods, and prepared all clothing and most other residential goods. After the autumn harvest, family deer-hunting parties ranged far into the forests, returning to their villages at midwinter. Spring runs of fish drew families to nearby streams and lake inlets.

Kinship and locality were the bases for traditional Iroquois political life. Iroquois speakers were fond of

Iroquois shoulder bag made of buckskin and decorated with porcupine quills and deer hair, c. 1750; in the Linden-Museum für Völkerkunde, Stuttgart, Ger. By courtesy of the Linden-Museum für Volkerkunde, Stuttgart, Germany.

meetings, spending considerable time in council. Council attendance was determined by locality, sex, age, and the specific question at hand. Each council had its own protocol and devices for gaining consensus, which was the primary mode of decision making.

The elaborate religious cosmology of the Iroquois was based on an origin tradition in which a woman fell from the sky. Other parts of the religious tradition featured deluge and earth-diver motifs, supernatural aggression and cruelty, sorcery, torture, cannibalism, star myths, and journeys to the otherworld. The formal ceremonial cycle consisted of six agricultural festivals featuring long prayers of thanks. There were also rites for sanctioning political activity, such as treaty making.

Warfare was important in Iroquois society, and, for men, self-respect depended upon achieving personal glory in war endeavours. War captives were often enslaved or adopted to replace dead family members. Losses to battle and disease increased the need for captives, who had become a significant population within Iroquois settlements by the late 17th century.

Early 21st-century population estimates indicated some 80,000 individuals of Iroquois-proper descent. When including the many Iroquois-speaking tribes, these estimates indicated more than 900,000 individuals.

MOHAWK

The Mohawk were the easternmost tribe of the Iroquois Confederacy. Their name for themselves is Kahniakehake, which means "people of the flint." Within the confederacy, they were known as the "keepers of the eastern door." At the time of European colonization, the Mohawk occupied three villages west of what is now Schenectady, N.Y.

Like the other Iroquois tribes, the Mohawk were semisedentary. Women engaged in maize (corn) agriculture. Men hunted during the fall and winter and fished during the summer. Related families lived together in longhouses, a symbol of Iroquois society. Each Mohawk community also had a local council that guided the village chief or chiefs.

According to some traditional accounts, the Mohawk visionary chief Dekanawida, who preached principles of peace, was instrumental in founding the Iroquois Confederacy. The Mohawk had nine representatives in the confederacy, three each from their Turtle, Wolf, and Bear clans. As with other Iroquois-speaking tribes, the Mohawk warred frequently against neighbouring Algonquian-speakers. The Dutch introduction of firearms during the fur trade increased the number of Mohawk victories. After contact with Europeans, however, the tribe diminished rapidly because of introduced diseases such as smallpox. Most Mohawk allied with the British in the French and Indian War, but some Catholic converts at mission settlements in Canada espoused the French cause and guided expeditions against their former alliance brothers.

During the American Revolution the Mohawk were pro-British. As the war concluded, they followed their leader Joseph Brant (Thayendanega) to Canada, where they have descendants at the Bay of Quinte and the Six Nations Indian Reserve at Brantford, Ont.

Mohawk leader Joseph Brant. At the conclusion of the American Revolution, Brant led the pro-British Mohawk out of the United States and into Canada. MPI/Archive Photos/Getty Images

Although they are involved in many professions, contemporary Mohawk people may be best known for their work on high steel construction projects, including the Empire State Building and the George Washington Bridge, both in New York City. For some individuals this dangerous work may represent a continuation of the Mohawk ideals of bravery and personal risk taking for the greater good.

Population estimates suggested some 47,000 Mohawk descendants in the early 21st century.

NEUTRAL

The Neutral lived in what are now southern Ontario, Can., and western New York, northeastern Ohio, and southeastern Michigan, U.S. The French came to call these allied tribes Neutre ("Neutral") because they remained neutral in the wars between the Iroquois Confederacy and the Huron before the mid-17th century. This neutrality did not extend to other tribes, however, and the early 17th century saw the Neutral alliance at war with groups to the west, particularly the Potawatomi. Neutral villages of bark-covered houses were situated on high, defensible ground. Their economy was based on agriculture, supplemented by game, which was plentiful in this area.

During the war between the Huron and the Iroquois Confederacy in 1648–49, the Neutral attempted to gain favour with the latter by seizing Huron individuals, including those who had sought refuge in Neutral communities. The Iroquois nevertheless attacked and destroyed the Neutral in 1650–51. The last mention of them as an independent group was a report in 1653 of 800 members of the tribe living in the vicinity of Detroit in what is now Michigan. The remainder appear to have been either killed or absorbed by the Iroquois.

ONEIDA

At the time of European contact, the Oneida were living in what is now central New York state. They are one of the original five nations of the Iroquois Confederacy. Like the other Iroquois tribes, the Oneida were semisedentary and practiced maize (corn) agriculture. Longhouses sheltered families related through maternal descent. The Oneida were divided into three clans, each having three representatives in the confederation. Each community also had a local council that guided its chief or chiefs. Their name for themselves, Oneyoteaka, means "people of the standing stone."

The least populous of the Iroquois confederates during the 17th century, the Oneida had only one palisaded town of 60 to 100 longhouses. It was destroyed by a French Canadian expedition in 1696. Thereafter the community divided into Oneida (Upper Castle) and Canawaroghere. In the early 18th century a village of North Carolina Tuscarora joined the Oneida, becoming the sixth nation of the Iroquois Confederacy. Their former enemies residing in the Carolinas became the targets of war parties for a generation.

The Oneida supported the colonists in the American Revolution and consequently felt the depredations of the pro-British Iroquois led by the Mohawk chief Joseph Brant. Oneida communities took shelter within American lines, and Oneida men served the fledgling American military as scouts. Returning to their homes after the war, they were compensated by the U.S. government for their losses and took in remnants of the Mohegan nation. In the following years the Oneida divided into factions resulting from disagreements over Quaker missions, traditional religion, and the sale of lands. By 1833 those who had not settled at Oneida on the Thames River in Ontario had immigrated to Green Bay, Wis. A few families remained at Oneida and Onondaga, N.Y.

Early 21st-century population estimates indicated approximately 23,000 individuals of Oneida descent, most living in Wisconsin, New York, and Ontario.

ONONDAGA

The Onondaga lived in what is now the state of New York. They traditionally inhabited villages of wood and bark longhouses occupied by related families. They moved these houses periodically to plant new fields, to seek fresh supplies of firewood, and to be nearer fish and game. They grew maize (corn), beans, squash, sunflowers, and tobacco. A council of adult males in each community guided the village chiefs.

The Onondaga tribe, one of the five original nations of the Iroquois Confederacy, was the political and geographical centre of the league. With 14 seats in the council, the Onondaga furnished the chairman and the archivist, who kept the records of transactions in wampum belts.

In the 18th century a sizable faction of Onondaga favouring the French interest migrated to Jesuit mission settlements along the St. Lawrence River. Another faction remained loyal to the British, and, upon the breakup of the Iroquois Confederacy after the American Revolution, a small party followed other members to Grand River in

HIAWATHA

Hiawatha, whose Ojibwa name means "He Makes Rivers," was a legendary chief (c. 1450) of the Onondaga, and Indian tradition attributes the formation of what became known as the Iroquois Confederacy to him. In his miraculous character, Hiawatha was the incarnation of human progress and civilization. He taught agriculture, navigation, medicine, and the arts, conquering by his magic all the powers of nature that war against humans. The story of Hiawatha is told in Henry Wadsworth Longfellow's *The Song of Hiawatha* (1855), a long poem, written in the metre of the Finnish national epic, the *Kalevala*, which enjoyed wide popularity.

what is now Ontario. The majority, however, remained in their ancestral valley.

Early 21st-century population estimates indicated some 4,000 individuals of Onondaga descent.

SENECA

The Seneca lived in what is now western New York state and eastern Ohio. They were the largest of the original five nations of the Iroquois Confederacy, in which they were represented by eight chiefs. In the autumn small parties of Seneca men left the villages for the annual hunt, returning about midwinter. Spring was the fishing season. Seneca women were responsible for the cultivation of maize (corn) and other vegetables.

American General John Sullivan confiscated the land of Seneca tribes that had supported the British during the American Revolution. The loss of land instigated several changes to the Seneca way of life. MPI/ Archive Photos/Getty Images

The Seneca used kinship to organize their society. Extended families linked through the maternal line lived together in longhouses. The tribe had eight clans. These were in turn organized into two equally sized groups, or moieties. The moieties had their own chiefs and served complementary roles in games, funerals, and ceremonies. Kinship rules mandated marriage between, not within, the moieties. Each community had a council of adult males who guided the moiety chiefs.

Warfare with other indigenous nations was frequent. To a greater extent than most other Northeast Indians, the Seneca recovered their losses by adopting whole towns of other tribes. During the 17th century, wars led to the expansion of the original Seneca territory between Seneca Lake and the Genesee River to include all of western New York state from Niagara south along the Allegheny River into Pennsylvania. Remote from colonial contact, secure in game and maize, the Seneca could field 1,000 warriors, equaling the combined strength of the rest of the Iroquois Confederacy.

Because the Seneca were allied with the British during the American Revolution, American Gen. John Sullivan destroyed their villages in 1779. In 1797, having lost much of their land, the Seneca secured 12 tracts as reservations. In 1848 the incompetence and corruption of the hereditary chiefs, in particular their surrender of tribal land to non-Indians, caused the Seneca to change their form of government to a republic.

Early 21st-century population estimates indicated some 16,000 individuals of Seneca descent.

SUSQUEHANNOCK

Also called Conestoga or Susquehanna, the Susquehannock traditionally lived in palisaded towns along the Susquehanna River in what are now New York, Pennsylvania, and Maryland. Little is known of Susquehannock political organization, but they are thought to have been subdivided into several subtribes and clans. The name may have referred originally to a confederacy of tribes. Like other Iroquoian tribes, they were semisedentary agriculturalists.

The Susquehannock were first described by Capt. John Smith, who explored the upper Chesapeake Bay area in 1608. Throughout the historical period they were at war with the Iroquois, who conquered them in 1676 and forced them to settle near the Oneida tribe in New York. They were later allowed to return to their former territory along the Susquehanna River. Epidemics steadily reduced their number (estimated to have been about 5,000 in 1600), and in 1763 many of the remaining Susquehannock were massacred by whites inflamed by accounts of an Indian war on the Pennsylvania frontier, several hundred miles away. Susquehannock descendants numbered more than 400 in the early 21st century.

TIONONTATI

The Tionontati lived in the mountains south of Nottawasaga Bay, in what are now Grey and Simcoe counties, Ontario. In 1616 they were visited by the French, who called them the Tobacco Nation because of their extensive cultivation of this plant. They also grew maize (corn), beans, squash, and sunflowers. All agricultural work was done by women except for the clearing of the fields for planting. Hunting and fishing were also practiced, although they were of lesser importance. At the time the Jesuits established a mission among them in 1640, the tribe comprised two clans and had nine villages. Civil chiefs and councils of elders guided the civil affairs of the villages. War chiefs were concerned with military matters.

When the Iroquois attacked the Huron in 1648–50, many Huron took refuge with the Tionontati. In 1649 the Iroquois attacked one of the principal Tionontati villages, massacred the inhabitants, and destroyed the mission. The Tionontati and the Huron abandoned their country and fled to the region southwest of Lake Superior. The two tribes became amalgamated and were known as the Wyandot (a corrupted form of the name Wendat).

WENDAT

The Wendat consisted of a confederacy of four Iroquois-speaking bands of the Huron nation—the Rock, Bear, Cord, and Deer bands—together with a few smaller communities that joined them at different periods for protection against the Iroquois Confederacy. When first encountered by Europeans in 1615, the Wendat occupied a territory, sometimes called Huronia, around what are now Lake Simcoe and Georgian Bay, Ontario, Can. Some of the Wendat villages, consisting of large bark-covered dwellings housing several families each, were palisaded for protection. Villages were situated near fields where the Wendat grew maize (corn), the staple of their diet, which they supplemented with fish and, to a lesser extent, game.

Weakened by diseases introduced by Europeans and unable to obtain as many firearms and ammunition as their enemies, the Wendat were destroyed by the Iroquois Confederacy in 1648–50, and the constituent tribes dispersed. The neighbouring Tionontati united with some Huron refugees and became known to the English as the Wyandot, a corrupted form of Wendat.

In the early 21st century, population estimates indicated some 3,500 Wendat descendants.

WENROHRONON

The name Wenrohronon means "people of the place of the floating film," probably after the oil spring at what is now Cuba, N.Y., where they lived. The oil was a highly regarded medicine for various ailments. Like other Iroquoian tribes, the Wenrohronon were traditionally semisedentary, cultivating maize (corn), hunting, and fishing for their livelihood. Each community was guided by a chief and a council of elders.

An alliance with the Neutral tribe protected the Wenrohronon from Iroquois predation until 1639, when the Neutral withdrew their support. This act and an epidemic, probably of smallpox, led some 600 Wenrohronon to flee to the Huron for refuge. Many died of hunger, exposure, exhaustion, and disease before reaching safety with the Huron, who welcomed the survivors. The remaining Wenrohronon, who may have numbered 1,500, were incorporated into the Neutral and were later destroyed with them by the Iroquois.

Chapter 4
SOUTHEAST INDIANS

The peoples known as Southeast Indians are those Native Americans who were living in the southeastern United States at the time of European contact. The boundaries of this culture area are somewhat difficult to delineate because the traditional cultures in the Southeast shared many characteristics with those from neighbouring regions. Thus, most scholars define the region's eastern and southern boundaries as the Atlantic Ocean and the Gulf of Mexico, although some assign the southern portion of aboriginal Florida to the circum-Caribbean culture area.

To the west the Southeastern peoples merge with those of the southern Plains Indians and the most easterly of the Southwest Indians. To the north the traditions of the Southeast gradually transition to those of the Northeast Indians. When discussed jointly, the Southeast and Northeast culture areas are referred to as the Eastern Woodlands. As mentioned previously, this term is sometimes confused with that of the Eastern Woodland cultures, a term that describes a group of prehistoric societies rather than a culture area per se.

CULTURAL TRADITIONS

What is known about Native American cultures of the Southeast comes from a bevy of sources. Archaeological artifacts, historical documents, and ethnographic/

Distribution of Southeast American Indian tribes.

linguistic studies are augmented by native folklore and traditional oral history.

Many cultural traditions reported by the earliest European explorers, such as the use of ceremonial mounds, the heavy reliance on maize (corn), and the importance of social stratification in some areas, were heavily influenced by the Mississippians, who maintained fine craft traditions and also engaged in long-distance trade throughout the Southeast and the surrounding culture areas. The ceremonial centre, Cahokia, was home to many thousands at its climax about 1100 CE (estimates range from 8,000 to 20,000 people). The Natchez are perhaps the best-known members of the Mississippian culture to survive relatively intact into the colonial period.

COMMUNITY ORGANIZATION

The picture of the Southeast that emerges at the time of first European contact is one of intensive cultural change. The final centuries before contact appear to have been a period of cultural leveling marked by considerable population movement, warfare, and the formation of chieftains. Early written reports describe the political organization of the Southeast as including independent villages, autonomous village clusters, and "tribelets," independent polities that recognized cultural connections with the other groups or polities within the same tribe. Perhaps most analogous to the many independent polities of the California Indians, tribelets generally ranged in size from about a hundred to a few thousand people, depending on the richness of locally available resources.

Generally speaking, each community was fairly autonomous. A village might be linked to others in the same area by ties of kinship, language, and shared cultural traditions. Nevertheless, each claimed sovereignty over its locale and was governed by its own religio-political chiefs (during peacetime) and a complementary group of war leaders (during periods of conflict). Superordinate control at the tribal level was generally avoided, although the consolidation of tribelets into larger coalescent groups and even the formation of intertribal confederacies occurred as European settlements spread in the region.

Over most of the Southeast, religio-political chieftainship was hereditary within certain lineages. The degree of chiefly power and authority varied, however, from the almost divine kingship of the Great Sun among the theocratic Natchez to the self-effacing status of the peacemaking, consensus-seeking *mico*s and *uku*s among the more egalitarian Choctaw, Creek, and Cherokee. In contrast, war leaders normally achieved their positions on the basis of personal accomplishment. They also tended to be active and assertive personalities and younger, by about a generation, than the hereditary or "peace" chiefs.

The complementarity of peace chiefs and war leaders and the occurrence of competitive activities between neighbouring groups—including ball games, hunting contests, and trading expeditions—imbued traditional social structures with a characteristic dualism. The peace chief held sway in the village, whereas the war leader was ascendant in areas external to the village. He had authority in the village itself only when it was under the threat of imminent attack. Young men adjusted their behaviour according to the context of war or peace. They also prepared for the psychological and physical rigours of battle through extensive rituals in which war and peace were symbolically represented by the colours red and white, respectively.

Dualism was also expressed in the organization of clans, subtribes, and villages into complementary pairs, which in turn were sometimes characterized as red or white. Member towns of the Creek Confederacy were sometimes ranked in terms of their tribal affiliations or on the basis of outcomes of lacrosse-like ball games between towns. The Caddo were said to have ranked their clans on the basis of the reputed strength of the totemic animal ancestor, creating a symbolic pecking order.

Social stratification was highly developed in some parts of the Southeast and insignificant in others. Although much has been written about the so-called caste systems among the tribes of the lower Mississippi, the Chitimachas appear to have been the only society to have possessed true castes in the sense of ranked groups that practiced strict endogamy, or marriage within the group. While not a caste system in the strict sense of the term, social stratification was nonetheless highly elaborated among the aboriginal inhabitants of Florida. Among the Timucua, for instance, the "king" enjoyed an elevated status considerably above that of his followers and was sometimes carried about in a litter. The Natchez social hierarchy included strict rules for marriage and social status. In other tribes, such as the Cherokee, stratification was relatively unimportant, although certain clans might possess special ceremonial prerogatives and recruitment to certain offices might be determined on the basis of clan.

LANGUAGE FAMILIES

Four language families are represented in the Southeast culture area: Muskogean, Siouan, Iroquoian, and Caddoan. Several languages with tenuous connections to each of these major language families also existed throughout the region.

The largest linguistic group, the Muskogean-speaking peoples, included the Choctaw, Chickasaw, Apalachee, Creek, Seminole, Alabama, Koasati, Hitchiti, and Mikasuki branches. Four tribes of the lower Mississippi valley—the Natchez, Chitimacha, Tunica, and Atakapa— spoke languages with a distant affinity to Muskogean. However, their languages show sufficient divergence from the main Muskogean languages and from each other to warrant semi-independent status as linguistic isolates.

The Tutelo, Biloxi, Ofo (Mosopelea), and Catawba spoke Siouan languages. These tribes were widely scattered and probably represent different prehistoric penetrations of Siouan speakers into the Southeast. The Yuchi language also demonstrates distant affinities to Siouan but is sufficiently distinctive to be classified as an isolate. Many small piedmont groups were probably Siouan-speaking peoples, but surviving data are insufficient to make definite identifications.

The Cherokee represent the sole speakers of an Iroquoian language in the Southeast, although the Iroquoian-speaking Tuscarora, Nottaway, and Meherrin, residing on the northerly margin of the region, are included in the Southeast in some culture area maps. The Caddoan speakers on the western boundary of the region belong to a distinctive language family that shows remote relationships to the Siouan and Iroquoian families.

The present status of the language spoken by the Timucua, once the predominant tribe of northern Florida, is problematic. Linguists have suggested that it is related to such diverse groups as the Muskogean, Siouan, Algonquian, and Arawakan families. Mobilian was an important trade language containing many Choctaw components and served as a lingua franca in the Mississippi valley.

AGRICULTURE, SUSTENANCE, AND DOMESTIC LIFE

Plentiful game and abundant arable land meant there were ample provisions for the burgeoning populace of the Southeast culture area at the time of European contact. In south Florida, indigenous tribes adopted an essentially subtropical maritime way of life.

The primary division of labour in the Southeast was by gender. Women were responsible for cultivating the fields, gathering wild plant foods, cooking and preserving food, taking care of young children and elders, and manufacturing cordage, baskets, pottery, clothing, and other goods. Men assumed duties associated with war, trade, and the hunt. They were often away from the community for extended periods of time. Men also assisted in the harvest, cleared the fields by girdling trees, and constructed houses and public buildings. Both genders manufactured ceremonial objects.

An engraving by Theodore deBry depicting the Powhatan village of Secoton—with plowed fields of crops—from "Admiranda Narratio ...," a 1580s publication detailing life in the Virginia colonies. The Bridgeman Art Library/Getty Images

The economic mainstay of the Southeast was maize. Several varieties were grown, including "little corn" (related to popcorn); flint, or hominy; and flour, or dent, corn. Some varieties were baked or roasted on the cob; some were boiled into a succotash, a dish of stewed maize and beans; and still others were pounded into hominy or cornmeal in wooden mortars made of large upright, partly hollowed logs. Domesticated varieties of beans and squash were also important in the diet, as were wild greens. Fields were prepared with mattocks and hoes and planted by punching holes in the ground with digging sticks, inserting seeds, and covering the holes with earth to form a mound about two feet (one-half metre) in diameter. In some areas the soil was instead hilled into a series of linear mounds or ridges some three feet (one metre) across. Typically, beans and squash were planted adjacent to the maize. The bean vines used maize stalks as trellises, while the broad leaves of squash shaded the soil, minimizing weed growth and conserving moisture. Most fields belonged to individual households, although some tribes also cultivated communal fields. Communally grown produce was given to chiefs for redistribution to the needy and for use in various ceremonies and festivals.

The importance of maize in the Southeast cannot be overemphasized. It provided a high yield of nutritious food with a minimal expenditure of labour. Further, maize, beans, and squash were easily dried and stored for later consumption. This reliable food base freed people for lengthy hunting, trading, and war expeditions. It also enabled a complex civil-religious hierarchy in which political, priestly, and sometimes hereditary offices and privileges coincided.

Other cultivated plants included the sunflower, which was processed for its oil; *Chenopodium* and orache (herbs from the goosefoot family), which produced starchy seeds and spinachlike greens; and tobacco. Many additional plants, such as wild grapes, plums, and perhaps walnut and pecan trees, were in a condition of incipient domestication. Indigenous peoples exerted some effect on the propagation of these plants but did not fully domesticate them. Other important plant foods included berries, nuts, acorns, potatoes, zamia roots (similar to turnips), amaranths and smilax (providing shoots and seeds), and maple and honey locust sap. Two species of holly (*Ilex cassine* and *I. vomitoria*) were ingredients in a special decoction, the "black drink," which was used to induce sweating and vomiting in ceremonial and medical contexts. The economic botany of the region also encompassed a vast array of plants used for cordage, clothing, dyes, fish poisons, medicines, building materials, and various tools and utensils.

Before European colonization, the only domesticated animal in the Southeast was the dog. In this region canines were used to a minor extent in hunting and as food but were probably most important as sentinels that warned of approaching strangers. In accounts of the Hernando de Soto expedition (1539–43), there are several references to small, fat, barkless dogs that were served to the Spanish visitors by their indigenous hosts. Some of the 300 or more trail hogs that were transported by de Soto to feed his troops escaped and became the ancestors of the modern razorback hog. The Spanish also brought horses to North America, but their use was primarily confined to the Southwest and Mexico. As a result, the Southeastern peoples generally obtained horses at a much later date, through trade with Plains tribes.

Most of the region teemed with wild game: deer, black bears, a forest-dwelling subspecies of bison, elks, beavers, squirrels, rabbits, otters, and raccoons. In Florida, turtles and alligators played an important part in subsistence. Wild turkeys were the principal fowl taken, but partridges, quail, and seasonal flights of pigeons, ducks, and geese also contributed to the diet. The feathers of eagles, hawks, swans, and cranes were highly valued for ornamentation, and in some tribes a special status was reserved for an eagle hunter.

In both salt and fresh waters a wide variety of fish were taken. Fishing equipment included weirs (underwater corrals or pens), traps, dip nets, dragnets, hooks and lines, bows and arrows, and spears. Botanical poisons were administered in ponds and sluggish or dammed streams, creating a rich harvest of stunned, but edible, fish. Coastal groups gathered oysters, clams, mussels, cockles, and crabs, while those residing in the interior collected freshwater mussels and crayfish.

The peoples of the Southeast altered the landscape significantly by girdling trees and by the controlled use of fire. These activities created large areas of secondary growth that favoured certain types of berry bushes and other useful plants. The presence of this secondary-growth flora was essential for supporting the large populations of browsing deer, squirrels, rabbits, and wild turkeys on which people depended for sustenance. These environmental changes, combined with hunting, probably accelerated the decline of the wood bison and in some places other species. In areas with intensive maize cultivation, such as the lower Mississippi, early European explorers reported that game animals were scarce. In the central Southeast, however, native groups maintained an equilibrated balance with nature.

INTERRELATIONS WITH OTHER CULTURE AREAS

Cultural and economic exchanges with native groups from the Northeast and Plains culture areas were common, mainly due to a lack of geographic barriers between the Southeast and these regions. Contact with indigenous groups at even greater distances also is suggested. There is evidence of overseas cultural connections with the Antilles, with the dominant direction of diffusion moving from the mainland to the islands. Pre-Columbian interaction with Mesoamerican Indians, while indirect, nonetheless introduced maize, beans, and squash to the Southeast. Many scholars maintain that the building of mounds and the use of certain symbolic motifs also derive from Mesoamerica, although some believe these were developed independently by the Mississippians and their predecessors. Culture traits such as the cane blowgun, double-weave basketry, fibre-tempered pottery, and certain musical, ritual, and mythological elements suggest at least limited contact with South American peoples as well.

MESOAMERICAN INDIANS

Distribution of Mesoamerican Indians.

The indigenous peoples inhabiting Mexico and Central America (roughly between latitudes 14° N and 22° N) are known as Mesoamerican Indians.

These cultures have a common origin in the pre-Columbian civilizations of the area. Most Mesoamerican peoples belong to one of three linguistic groups: the Mayan, the Oto-Manguean, or the Uto-Aztecan. Mayan peoples, with the exception of a northeastern enclave, the Huastecs, live at the southeastern extremity of Mesoamerica. Oto-Mangueans are to be found in a wide area of Mesoamerica between Uto-Aztecan peoples to the north and east and Mayan and other peoples to the south. Oto-Manguean languages (now extinct) were spoken south of the Mayan area along the Pacific coasts of El Salvador, Honduras, and Nicaragua; and one Oto-Manguean language, North Pame, spoken in the central desert of highland Mexico, is outside Mesoamerica to the north. The main branches of the Oto-Manguean family are the Western, including Oto-Pamean, Chinantecan, Subtiaba-Tlapanecan, and Manguean; and the Eastern, including Popolocan, Zapotecan, Amuzgoan, and Mixtecan. As a result of the expansion of the Aztec empire centred in the Valley of Mexico, Uto-Aztecan enclaves are found throughout the area. Tarascan, a language now considered to be a language isolate, is spoken in the highlands of Michoacán, Mexico.

As each household in the Southeast was fairly self-sufficient, the economic specializations and trade networks that developed tended to centre on subsidiary and luxury items. For instance, as salt deposits were unequally distributed, salt became an important trade item. There was regular trade between the coast and the interior. Shells, which were used for beads and pendants and to decorate ritual objects, were exchanged for soapstone, flint, furs, and other inland resources. Pottery made with distinctive types of red clay and artifacts made of native copper suggest important trade connections with the western Great Lakes groups that controlled the locales where these raw materials were found.

VILLAGES, TOWNS, AND DWELLINGS

Native villages and towns, of various sizes and configurations, were present throughout the Southeast. The typical village was home to 500 or fewer residents, although towns with populations exceeding 1,000 were not unknown. Two types of settlement patterns predominated. Dispersed hamlets, each of which might contain storage buildings and a special cookhouse in addition to one or more dwellings, were arrayed along the valley bottoms or the course of streams. In contrast were tightly nucleated settlements, often surrounded with protective timber palisades. Usually each group of hamlets was associated with a palisaded town, where the community as a whole gathered for celebrations and ritual events.

In general, settlements were semipermanent and located near rich alluvial soil or, in the lower Mississippi region, near natural levees. Such land was easily tilled, possessed adequate drainage, and enjoyed renewable productivity. Fertility was enhanced by burning off any stalks

A Timucua village, engraving by Theodor de Bry from a drawing by Jacques Le Moyne, c. 1564; first published in 1591. Library of Congress, Washington, D.C.

or vines that remained from the previous harvest. The length of the growing season in the Southeast allowed many fields to be planted twice each year. The first planting was done in spring, and some produce was available by midsummer, when a second planting was undertaken. The major harvest time, in late summer and early fall, was a time of plenty during which most of the major ceremonies were celebrated. Many villages emptied somewhat during the winter months, when households took to the woods in search of game. Individuals with limited mobility, however, would remain at home. Men also undertook a shorter hunt in late spring and early summer, after the first crops had been planted.

The heart of a town was typically a ceremonial centre. This centre consisted of several elements. A council house or temple in the interior region might be semisubterranean or located on an earthen mound. A central plaza or square, among the Muskogean speakers, was usually surrounded by three or four benches or arbours oriented in the cardinal directions. A ball pole or scalp post was sometimes topped with a carved animal emblem. The residences of the chief and other important local dignitaries were also part of the centre, as were granaries or other structures for storing communal produce.

Considerable variation in house types existed. In much of the region, people built circular, conical-roofed winter "hot houses" that were sealed tight except for an entryway and smoke hole. Summer dwellings tended to be rectangular, gabled, thatch-roofed structures made from a framework of upright poles and walled with wattle and daub. To the south, especially from the early 19th century onward, houses often had raised floors, palmetto-thatched roofs, and open sides. To the west, the Caddoans lived in domed grass houses.

WATTLE AND DAUB

In the wattle-and-daub method of building construction, vertical wooden stakes, or wattles, are woven with horizontal twigs and branches, and then daubed with clay or mud. It is an ancient and widespread technique and is one of the oldest known ways to weatherproof a structure. In England, Iron Age sites have been discovered with remains of circular dwellings constructed in this way, the staves being driven into the earth.

When this method is used as filling-in for a timber-framed structure the wattles are set into holes bored in a horizontal timber above and fitted into a groove in a corresponding timber below. Then the staves are woven with twigs and plastered with clay. The half-timbered houses of medieval Europe were frequently finished this way. The lath-and-plaster method of building up interior walls, which was common before the introduction of such materials as plasterboard and Sheetrock, is a more modern evolution of the wattle-and-daub technique, using standardized materials.

FAMILIAL AND SPOUSAL RELATIONSHIPS

Almost all indigenous peoples in the Southeast culture area traced their heritage through matrilineal lines. Kinship was determined via clans formed and held together on the basis of a singular ancestor or totem reckoned through the mother. For those groups that had them, clans were usually dispersed throughout a tribe or nation rather than limited to a particular village or tribelet. This arrangement provided a kind of social adhesive that crosscut and bound together the larger body politic. For instance, clan members were generally expected to offer hospitality to clan kin from other villages. Certain ritual knowledge and ceremonial privileges were also customarily passed down along clan lines. In addition, clans were important as mechanisms of social control, as vengeance for serious crimes was frequently a clan responsibility.

Marriage was often marked by a symbolic ceremonial exchange whereby the groom presented the bride with game and the bride reciprocated with plant food. Residence after marriage was normally established in the wife's natal household. The husband was expected to contribute to the economic maintenance of his wife's family as a form of bride service and to prove his abilities as a provider. After a few years the couple might leave to form their own household. Most tribes permitted (and some encouraged) premarital sexual intimacy. After marriage, however, adultery—especially on the part of the wife—could be severely punished. In contrast, divorce seems to have been a frequent and almost casual event. Polygyny, a form of marriage in which wives share a husband, was permitted in most groups. Usually new partners could not join the marriage without the consent of all the extant partners. The levirate, a custom by which a widow marries her deceased husband's brother, was fairly common. Because it was a method for ensuring that each woman and her children had a male provider, levirate marriages increased with the heightened male mortality that resulted when tribes resisted colonial conquest.

The French described the elaborate rank system of the Natchez as being considerably entwined with marriage and kin customs. Natchez social hierarchy was divided into four groups: three upper classes composed hierarchically of the suns, the nobles, and the honoured people, and a lower class of commoners (whom the early French sources refer to as "stinkards"). Members of the upper classes were required to marry members of the commoner class. Many commoners also married other commoners. The offspring of upper-class men would assume a rank one step below that of their fathers. For example, the child of a sun father and commoner mother would become a member of the noble class. The children of upper-class women, however, retained the rank of their mothers. Interestingly, the system described by the French would have been unstable, as all women would have been born into the upper classes after several generations. Many explanations have been advanced to explain this "Natchez paradox," but the problem probably originated in the inaccuracies or incompleteness of the original French sources.

RAISING AND EDUCATING FUTURE GENERATIONS

Care and protection of children in Southeastern native cultures began in utero. Late in a woman's pregnancy, in anticipation of the child's arrival, both she and the father adopted a specialized diet and faced restrictions on their activities. Children nursed until they self-weaned or the mother again became pregnant. The child's early education was the responsibility of the mother. As they grew older, girls were trained in duties such as the growing, preserving, and storing of food, receiving instruction from their mothers and other female relatives. Boys received instruction from their fathers and their uncles on their mother's side of the family. In many systems the mother's eldest brother, as the senior male in the matrilineage, assumed considerable importance as a disciplinarian, tutor, and sponsor for his sister's son.

A 19th-century Choctaw encampment along the Mississippi River. Women of the Southeastern tribes taught young girls how to cook and preserve food. MPI/Archive Photos/Getty Images

Behaviour considered proper was reinforced with praise and encouragement, as when a boy killed his first deer or a girl completed her first basket. Behaviour considered improper was usually greeted mildly. Preferred responses ranged from gentle ribbings, rebukes, and ridicule to shame. Children were rarely subjected to physical punishment. In those few instances in which corporal punishment was deemed necessary, it was generally meted out by someone other than the parents. A popular method of chastisement throughout the Southeast was the raking of the skin with briars or a special pointed scratching instrument, but generally such action was regarded as strengthening or toughening the child rather than as delivering direct retribution for misdeeds. Boys enjoyed considerable permissiveness and spent much of their time with their peers. Common activities included wrestling, playing games imitative of adult activities, and stalking rabbits, squirrels, and birds with blowguns or scaled-down bows and arrows. Girls, in contrast, were subject to close surveillance and assumed household responsibilities from an early age.

Puberty rituals were either absent or relatively undeveloped in the Southeast. Girls were secluded at menarche, but this event occasioned no public celebration. All women were provided with a few days of seclusion and rest during menstruation. Similarly, no special rituals attended the transition from boyhood to manhood. A boy might receive instructions from tribal elders in esoteric lore or in preparation for special ritual offices, but the completion of such training was seldom marked by a formal commencement. A young man's first participation in a war party and the achievement of military honours were, however, given public recognition. Probably the clearest markers of the passage from adolescence to adulthood were marriage and the birth of one's first child.

RELIGION AND SPIRITUALITY

As in the Northeast, animism—where humans share the physical world with the spirits of the dead and the yet-to-be born, as well as living and abiotic elements such as mountains and clouds—was a central focus of Southeastern belief systems. Animals in particular were thought to have souls and hold sway over the human populace. Slain animals sought vengeance against humanity through the agency of their "species chief," a supernatural animal with great power. The Deer Chief, for instance, was able to exact revenge on humans who dishonoured his people—the deer—during the hunt. Hunting thus became a sacred act and was much imbued with taboo, ritual, and sacrifice. Most disease was attributed to failures in placating the souls of slain animals.

The plant world was considered friendly to humans, and the Cherokee thought that every animal-sent disease could be cured by a corresponding plant antidote. The economic significance of maize was memorialized by the near universality of the Green Corn ceremony, or Busk, throughout the Southeast. This was a major ceremonial suffused with an ethos of annual renewal in which the sacred fire—and often the hearth fires of each home—was rekindled. Old debts and grudges were forgiven and forgotten, old clothing and stored food were discarded, and a sense of community was regenerated.

Spiritual power could reside in objects other than plants and animals. Medicine men possessed sacred stones, quartz crystals, and other mystically endowed paraphernalia. Other objects were consecrated to symbolize the collective solidarity of the group. The Cherokee made use of a palanquin or litter within which were placed revered objects; the Tukabahchee Creek possessed sacred embossed copper plates; and the temples of several Lower Mississippi tribes contained an assortment of idols and icons. Natural objects could be infused with sacred power in a variety of ways, including contact with thunder, as in lightning-struck wood, immersion in a rapidly flowing stream, and exposure to the smoke of the sacred fire or of ritually prepared tobacco.

The outlines of a formal theology can be discerned from early accounts of some of the stratified societies and from those tribes that survived the immediate ravages of European contact. Most groups possessed origin myths, often involving a primal deluge into which prototypical beings plunged to secure a portion of mud that magically expanded to create the Earth, which was often viewed as an island. The subsequent course of mythological history was frequently related in terms of a cosmic struggle between a celestial culture hero who bestowed boons on

MEDICINE MEN

The term *medicine man* has been used most widely in the context of American Indian cultures, though it is widely used in other cultures as well. Because women perform this function in many societies, other terms, such as *medicine person* or *healer*, are also employed. These healers are knowledgeable about the magical and chemical potencies of various substances (medicines) and skilled in the rituals through which they are administered.

Traditionally, medicine people are called upon to prevent or heal the physical and mental illnesses of individuals as well as the social ruptures that occur when murders and other calamitous events take place within a community. Some medicine men and women undergo rigorous initiation to gain supernormal powers, while others become experts through apprenticeships. Many complete a combination of these processes.

The medicine person commonly carries a kit of objects— feathers of particular birds, suggestively shaped or marked stones, pollen, hallucinogenic or medicinal plants, and other items—that are associated with healing. In some cases these materials are considered to have been drawn out of the body of the practitioner at his or her initiation to the healer's arts. Correspondingly, the work of healing often involves the extraction of offending substances from the patient's body by sucking, pulling, or other means. In some cases an object must be physically removed from the patient (e.g., the healer removes a projectile from a wound). In cases where the nature of the offending substance is metaphysical, however, the healing ritual focuses on achieving mental and spiritual health. In such cases a symbolic object may be "removed" from the patient by sleight of hand.

humankind and an underworld antihero who became the source of the fatality and misfortune inherent in the human condition. Southeastern myths and folktales are populated by myriad nature spirits, monsters, tricksters, giants, and little people.

Among many tribes, evidence survives that suggests belief in a supreme being, sometimes depicted as the master of breath. This ultimate divinity was frequently associated with the sun and its earthly aspect, fire. In addition, the world was viewed as quadrisected by the cardinal directions. Each direction had a presiding spirit and appropriate colour symbolism. Concern with the remote supreme being seems to have rested more with the priesthood than with the everyday activities of the average individual. The life of the latter was more intimately tied up with the proximal spiritual beings who were felt to intervene more directly in human affairs.

In some of the wealthier stratified societies, priests were given specialized training and became full-time religious practitioners responsible for the spiritual health of the community. Priests also assumed the responsibility of conducting the major collective religious rituals that punctuated the calendrical cycle. Complementary to the priesthood were various individual magico-medical practitioners, such as sorcerers, conjurors, diviners, herbalists, and healers, who were generally part-time specialists and catered to individual needs and crises, especially the treatment of illness. Medical therapy was intricately enmeshed in the spiritual view of the world and might include such practical procedures as isolation, sweating, bathing, bloodletting, sucking, the inducement of vomiting, the internal and external application of herbal medicines, and the recitation of ritual chants.

The frequent elaboration of funerary practices, including interring the chiefly dead with great quantities of freshwater pearls and other rare materials, indicates that most groups believed in an afterlife. It was generally thought that the souls of the recently deceased would hover around the community and try to induce close friends and relatives to join them in their journey to eternity. Thus, the elaborate funerary rites and the extensive taboos associated with death were as much a protection for the living as a commemoration of the dead. This was especially the case because death was never considered a natural event but was always the result of malevolent animal spirits, witches, or the deadly machinations of sorcerers. If a death had been caused by human agents, the soul of the deceased would never rest until vengeance had been secured by its living relatives. Once appeased, the soul moved to a final resting place, the location of which varied from group to group. Typically, this was either in the direction of the setting sun, in the celestial firmament, or in a non-hellish part of the underworld.

Chapter 5
EUROPEAN COLONIZATION AND THE SOUTHEAST CULTURE AREA

The farming groups that were encountered by the first Europeans to visit the continent were more sedentary than their predecessors had been, but they continued to engage in hunting. Agriculturists' housing and settlements tended to be more substantial than those of Archaic groups, and their communities were often protected by walls or ditches. Many also developed hierarchical systems of social organization.

The arrival of European explorers and settlers altered native life in the Southeast—sometimes for the better but mainly for worse. Conquest, trade, attempted religious conversion, and the forced removal of Native Americans from their land all played a role in shaping the culture of the indigenous people of this region for centuries.

THE 1500S: EUROPEAN EXPLORATION AND CONQUEST

Although permanent colonial settlements were not established in the region until 1565, when the Spanish founded Saint Augustine in present-day Florida, the native peoples of the Southeast suffered greatly due to European exploration during the 16th century. The earliest expeditions, by Juan Ponce de Léon (1513, 1521) and Panfilo de Narváez (1528; best known for the narrative produced by Álvar Núñez Cabeza de Vaca), were short-lived but exposed indigenous peoples to the devastating effects of European diseases, such as smallpox, to which they had not been previously exposed. Epidemics soon decimated the native population. Mortality rates for these nonimmune populations are estimated to have been as high as 50 to 90 percent; these rates generally combine deaths due directly to disease with those resulting from subsidiary causes, such as famine.

SMALLPOX

Once one of the world's most dreaded plagues, smallpox is an acute infectious disease caused by the virus *Variola major,* a member of the orthopoxvirus family. The disease has been known for thousands of years—it was described as early as 1122 BCE in China and is referred to in the ancient Sanskrit texts of India. Evidence of smallpox was found on the mummified head of the Egyptian pharaoh Ramses V, who died in approximately 1156 BCE.

Smallpox is spread by inhaling saliva or mucus droplets from an infected individual. After about 7 to 17 days, flulike symptoms begin. These include high fever, body aches, and fatigue. Within a few days a body rash develops that quickly evolves into pus-filled blisters, or pustules. By the second week the pustules form crusts, which dry out and turn into scabs. After a week or so the scabs fall off, leaving deep and often disfiguring scars.

The overall mortality rate of smallpox is high—up to 30 percent of its victims die from the disease. Those who do not die may suffer from complications of the disease, which include blindness, pneumonia, and kidney damage. No adequate treatment is available to fight the virus, though antibiotics may be prescribed to hinder secondary bacterial infections. The virus is remarkably stable and can exist in the environment and on bedding and clothing for extended periods of time.

Large outbreaks of smallpox have occurred throughout history, affecting individuals from all walks of life. In addition to outbreaks that devastated many Native American tribes, smallpox was responsible for the deaths of Queen Mary II of England, Emperor Joseph I of Austria, King Luis I of Spain, Tsar Peter II of Russia, Queen Ulrika Elenora of Sweden, and King Louis XV of France.

A vaccine for the disease was discovered in 1796 by Edward Jenner, an English physician. Although Jenner's vaccine was effective, it was not used consistently. By the 1950s, roughly 50 million cases of smallpox still occurred worldwide each year. By the end of the 20th century, the disease was eradicated, thanks to a worldwide vaccination campaign. The possibility of the virus being used as an agent of bioterrorism or in biological warfare has since become an increasing threat.

Hernando de Soto, who had proved instrumental in the conquest of the Inca (1532), was eventually commissioned by Spain to conquer La Florida. From 1539 to 1543 his expedition traveled through what are now the states of Florida, Georgia, South Carolina, North Carolina, Tennessee, Alabama, Mississippi, Arkansas, and Louisiana. Some Southeastern tribes greeted de Soto as they would a paramount chief, offering food, tribute of pearls and copper, sexual access to women, and porters. Other towns in de Soto's path attacked the expedition. However, as the Spanish group included some 600–700 heavily armed professional soldiers, the conquistadors' counteroffenses left few settlements intact.

By the close of the 16th century, several factors had combined to disrupt traditional life in the Southeast. Thousands of individuals were killed during direct warfare with explorers. European diseases caused thousands more deaths. The subsidiary effects of these losses further devastated the Southeast: groups with too few people to plant and hunt were forced into starvation or refugee status. Much practical and ritual knowledge was lost, and indigenous political structures were weakened. The final and perhaps least well-known factor was the trade in indigenous slaves, who were generally captured by rival tribelets and sold to the Spanish for export to New England, the Caribbean, and elsewhere. Many groups on

Native Americans assist Spaniard Hernando de Soto (on horse) *in Florida. Some tribes treated Europeans with respect, even reverence, while others were openly hostile to those they considered dangerous interlopers.* Archive Photos/Getty Images

the coast and in the piedmont lost their political or social viability during this period. Their surviving members generally became part of larger, more powerful tribes such as the Choctaw, Cherokee, or various member tribes of the Creek Confederacy.

MISSIONIZATION IN THE 1600S

Trade with the Europeans picked up steam during the 17th century. Southeast native peoples found a market for their animal skins, particularly deer. The demand was equally high for European firearms, which the native peoples used for hunting and protection. European exploration of the inland Southeast generally ceased, and colonial settlement began in earnest on the coasts.

The most important development in this century, however, was the establishment of missions and the propagation of Roman Catholicism among native peoples. Jesuits attempted to missionize coastal Georgia and South Carolina in 1565–66 but abandoned those areas

after several friars were killed. Spain replaced the Jesuits with Franciscans in 1573. By 1700 more than 100 missions had been established in northern Florida and southern Georgia, particularly among the Timucua, Guale, and Apalachee peoples. Reports to Spain describe these groups as almost entirely Christianized by 1670.

The Southeastern missions drew (or were assigned) fewer Spanish soldiers and civilians than missions in other areas. Their absence allowed the friars to

Artwork showing a Jesuit missionary baptizing a Native American infant. Missions sprang up throughout the Southeast as European factions attempted to Christianize the so-called "heathens." MPI/Archive Photos/ Getty Images

proceed with their work unhindered by the rapes, kid-
nappings, and beatings that such individuals commonly
visited upon native peoples elsewhere. The indigenous
power structures of the region had been weakened, and
the surviving hereditary chiefs and war leaders had proved
incapable of ending the losses caused by disease, warfare,
and slavery. As they were accustomed to accepting leadership that combined religion and politics, many people
realized that allying themselves with the Franciscans
would afford a measure of protection against further
military and slaving raids. They may have also hoped
that the presence of a new deity would bring some relief
from disease. Finally, the friars themselves were careful
to limit their mandate to those aspects of culture that
were overtly religious, such as baptism and attendance at
mass. Other aspects were left alone and might incorpo-
rate Christianity (or not) depending upon the wishes of
a given community. Among the Apalachee, for instance,
the late-summer Busk quickly incorporated celebrations
of the feast day of San Luis Rey, which occurred at the
same time of year.

In 1706 the last missions were abandoned because of
the conflicts that were arising between Europe's imperial
powers. However, the friars' work was enduring. During
the 20th century, many indigenous groups from the
Southeast persisted in practicing more or less syncretic
religions that combined indigenous and Catholic practices, as well as preparing the ground for later conversion
to Protestant sects.

TERRITORIAL CONFLICTS OF THE 1700S

As the 1700s approached, armed conflicts arose in an
effort to determine supremacy and control, both in

KING WILLIAM'S WAR

The North American extension of the War of the Grand Alliance, waged by William III of Great Britain and the League of Augsburg against France under Louis XIV, is known as King William's War. It was fought from 1689 to 1697 by Canadian and New England colonists. Because of the importance of Indian participation, this conflict is also known as the first of the four French and Indian Wars.

The colonists divided in support of their mother countries and, together with their respective Indian allies, assumed primary responsibility for their own defense. The British, led by Sir William Phips, captured Port Royal, Acadia (later Nova Scotia), but failed to take Quebec. The French and Indians, under the Count de Frontenac, carried out successful attacks on Schenectady, N.Y., Salmon Falls (in present New Hampshire), and Casco Bay (in present Maine) but failed against their main target—Boston. The protracted war ended with the Treaty of Rijswijk (1697).

Europe and in North American territories. By dint of their occupation of the land in America and allegiances formed through trade channels, the indigenous peoples of the Southeast (and the Northeast) found themselves increasingly drawn into these foreign struggles. Local theatres of war and their instigating European conflicts included King William's War (1689–97) and Europe's War of the Grand Alliance (1689–97); Queen Anne's War (1702–13) and the War of the Spanish Succession (1701–14); King George's War (1744–48) and the War of the Austrian Succession (1740–48); and the French and Indian War (1754–63) and the Seven Years' War (1756–63). The American Revolution (1775–83), in which France, Spain, and the Netherlands supported the colonies in their fight against England, was yet another conflict with at least some origins in European politics.

By the early 18th century many smaller indigenous groups had merged with larger tribes, and especially with major groups such as the Creek, Chickasaw, Choctaw, and Cherokee. Each of these large polities engaged in alliances with the European powers, and they often found themselves pitted against one another. Indigenous communities soon realized that trade and diplomatic relations with Spain, France, and England were intertwined and could be manipulated to their advantage. The Creek found it especially profitable to set the three imperial powers against one another.

By mid-century, however, the Southeastern Indians' ascendancy in trade, military might, and diplomacy was being overshadowed by an increasing mass of European immigrants. Many were fleeing homelands torn by war. Some were fleeing religious persecution. Still others sought to escape depressed economies or were transported as punishment for petty crimes. The colonizing population in the Southeast alone had grown from perhaps 50,000 Europeans in 1690 to approximately 1 million individuals by 1790. The enslaved African population in the region grew from about 3,000 to 500,000 during the same period.

Previous colonizers had built most of their settlements near the swampy, malarial wetlands of the Atlantic and Gulf coasts. Most Southeastern peoples found these locations relatively undesirable. As coastal locales could not support the enormous increase in European and African populations, an inland development boom ensued. This ultimately proved more dangerous to the Southeastern tribes than epidemics or war.

THE 1800S: EUROPEAN ENCROACHMENT AND FORCED REMOVAL

At the dawn of the 19th century, the Southeastern peoples were culturally blended, having adopted certain European customs and practices while maintaining many of their own traditions as well. This strategy allowed tribes of the Southeast culture area to become the owners of large, prosperous farms and plantations. These were almost all members of the Creek, Cherokee, Choctaw, or Chickasaw tribes, who with the Seminole became known as the Five Civilized Tribes. The Seminole were a multiethnic group that included Creek and other native refugees who had fled the mid-18th-century conflicts, as well as Africans and African Americans who had escaped slavery.

The desire of the burgeoning Euro-American population to acquire land was fierce. As the pressure to cede land to settlers increased, the tribes opted to negotiate with the nascent United States in the belief that treaties and other agreements would be enforced by this government, as they had by Spain, England, and France. The settlers' desire for more land and their envy at indigenous prosperity caused them to agitate for oppressive Indian policies. Violence eventually erupted in the form of the Seminole Wars. The first war (1817–18) was fought in part to defend individuals of African descent from capture and a return to enslavement. American forces led by Andrew Jackson invaded northern Florida, kidnapped a few individuals, and destroyed many Seminole settlements. In response, the tribe moved south and rebuilt their society.

The Cherokee preferred to use legal strategies to maintain their property and the political independence

Massacre of the Whites by the Indians and Blacks in Florida, *wood-cut from* An Authentic Narrative of the Seminole War, *by Daniel F. Blanchard, 1836.* Library of Congress, Washington, D.C.

guaranteed them by treaty. Sequoyah's 1821 invention of a syllable-based writing system for the Cherokee language enabled the wide circulation of a draft Cherokee constitution. Tribal members voted to adopt the new constitution in 1827. At the same time, settler agitation regarding the primacy of state versus tribal sovereignty was accelerated by the discovery of gold within the Cherokee Nation lands, and the Georgia legislature in turn passed a law extending state authority to tribal lands. Many Euro-Americans felt that tribes should not be allowed to maintain separate governments within state boundaries. Instead, they proposed that tribal members choose between regular citizenship or tribal sovereignty. Indians could either give up the protections provided by treaty agreements or remove themselves to territories outside the states. The Cherokee saw this as a vacuous argument, as their sovereign status was clearly delineated in the treaties they had negotiated with the federal government. They chose to file suit against the state in federal court.

While the Cherokee lawsuit moved through the judicial system, the United States Congress passed the Indian Removal Act (1830). This enabled the government to

INDIAN REMOVAL ACT

The Indian Removal Act (May 28, 1830) was the first major legislative departure from the U.S. policy of officially respecting the legal and political rights of the American Indians. The act authorized the president to grant Indian tribes unsettled western prairie land in exchange for their desirable territories within state borders (especially in the Southeast), from which the tribes would be removed. The rapid settlement of land east of the Mississippi River made it clear by the mid-1820s that the white settlers would not tolerate the presence of even peaceful Indians there. Pres. Andrew Jackson (1829–37) vigorously promoted this new policy, which became incorporated in the Indian Removal Act of 1830. Although the bill provided only for the negotiation with tribes east of the Mississippi on the basis of payment for their lands, trouble arose when the United States resorted to force to gain the Indians' compliance with its demand that they accept the land exchange and move west.

A number of northern tribes were peacefully resettled in western lands considered undesirable for white settlers. The problem lay in the Southeast, where members of what were known as the Five Civilized Tribes (Chickasaw, Choctaw, Seminole, Cherokee, and Creek) refused to trade their cultivated farms for the promise of strange land in the Indian Territory with a so-called permanent title to that land. Many of these Indians had homes, representative government, children in missionary schools, and trades other than farming. Some 100,000 tribesmen were forced to march westward under U.S. military coercion in the 1830s. Up to 25 percent of the Indians, many in manacles, perished en route. The trek of the Cherokee in 1838–39 became known as the infamous "Trail of Tears." Even more reluctant to leave their native lands were the Florida Indians, who fought resettlement for seven years (1835–42) in the second of the Seminole Wars.

The frontier began to be pushed aggressively westward in the years that followed, upsetting the "guaranteed" titles of the displaced tribes and further reducing their relocated holdings.

designate as Indian Territory land in the trans-Mississippi West. It created a process through which land in the new territory would be exchanged for tribal land in the East and provided funds for the transportation of tribes to the new domain.

The native peoples of the Southeast responded in different ways to the realpolitik of this event. The Choctaw agreed to removal relatively quickly, hoping to leave the conflict behind them. Federal corruption and incompetence ensured that their journey was poorly provisioned, however. Inadequate food, sanitation, shelter, and transport caused many deaths.

In the meantime, *Cherokee Nation* v. *Georgia* had made its way to the United States Supreme Court. In 1831 the Court decided that indigenous peoples living within the United States were no longer independent nations and that as a domestic sovereign nation—in other words, one that depended upon the United States to uphold its political independence—the Cherokee had no right to sue in the federal court system.

A related suit, *Worcester* v. *Georgia*, involved a Euro-American missionary who refused to take a state loyalty oath and visited native property without the necessary state permit. The Supreme Court decision, made in 1832, stated that the right to regulate tribal affairs was exclusive to the federal government—states had no similar right to extend their laws to the tribes. President Andrew Jackson refused to enforce the *Worcester* decision. This allowed the states to enact further legislation damaging to the tribes. Notably, these two cases have formed the basis for most subsequent Indian law in the United States.

The Creek agreed to removal in 1832, but delays in their departure resulted in great hardship on their journey westward. A few Seminole leaders signed an agreement of removal in 1832, but the majority of tribal members declared that the agreement was not binding and refused to go. This provoked the Second Seminole War (1835–42), a conflict that the Seminole eventually lost, with many being forcibly removed to the west.

Learning of the hardships suffered by other indigenous groups, most of the Chickasaw tribelets took matters into their own hands. Many of these groups sold their land at a profit and moved west in the late 1830s. Having for the most part planned, provisioned, and paid for the journey themselves, they fared better than other tribes. Their journey was difficult nonetheless, and they suffered many casualties from smallpox and malnourishment.

Most Cherokee refused to depart, and many were forced from their homes at gunpoint beginning in 1837. In

Artist Robert Ottokar Lindneux's interpretation of the Trail of Tears—the forced removal of several Southeastern tribes from their homes to a reservation in present-day Oklahoma.© SuperStock

the most infamous of the forced relocations conducted under the Removal Act, some 15,000 Cherokee were evicted and marched westward on a harrowing journey causing the deaths of some 4,000 of their people.

The Removal Act was enforced throughout the Eastern Woodlands, and few native individuals remained there after 1840. Notable exceptions include groups of Seminole in Florida; the Eastern band of Cherokee in North Carolina; some Catawba and many Lumbee in the piedmont area of North and South Carolina; the Poarch Creek in eastern Alabama; the Mississippi Choctaw; the Tunica and Chitimacha of Louisiana; small remnant groups in the coastal Carolinas; and, scattered throughout the Southeast, innumerable unrecognized groups claiming Indian descent. In all, historical demographers estimate that some 100,000 people from the Eastern Woodlands were forced from their homelands and that some 15,000 died while on what has become known as the Trail of Tears.

THE QUEST TO REGAIN SOVEREIGNTY

The surviving members of the Five Civilized Tribes set about trying to rebuild their economies in Indian Territory (present-day Oklahoma). As had been the case in their home territory, many families turned to farming; other service-related jobs, such as blacksmithing, also brought in money.

The start of the American Civil War put the brakes on the economic revitalization of the indigenous peoples of the Southeast. Since Indian Territory was surrounded by states committed to the war, members of the Five Civilized Tribes and other displaced Native Americans found themselves directly in harm's way, suffering at the hands of both Union and Confederate forces. People were assaulted, farms and outbuildings burned, and crops and livestock stolen, destroyed, or dispersed. After the war, the tribes worked to rebuild their communities yet again. The United States, having allowed indigenous owners to retain slaves during removal, now insisted that all former slaves be freed and recognized as official members of the tribes of their owners. Known as freedmen, this population experienced various phases of acceptance and rejection from others in the Native American community, and their status remained controversial in the early 21st century.

During Reconstruction (1865–77), conflicts in the West resulted in the movement of a large number of displaced Plains tribes and others from their traditional homelands to Indian Territory. The United States took land assigned to groups already resident in the territory and transferred it to the newcomers. By the 1890s, continued Euro-American land hunger had resulted in allotment, a federal policy under which land held in common by tribes was divided into parcels and dispersed. Each indigenous head of household was assigned a parcel, as were orphans and a few other categories of individuals. The remaining land was made available to settlers, railroads, and others for development. Although the Five Civilized Tribes were immune from the initial enforcement of the new policy because they held clear title to their property, an act of Congress brought them under allotment jurisdiction in 1898. Like the other indigenous residents of the territory, they lost tens of thousands of acres.

Under policies initiated in 1906, indigenous peoples lost the right to elect their own tribal governments, which were replaced by federally appointed chiefs and tribal councils. The administration of schools and other institutions formerly managed by the tribes of Indian Territory also devolved to the United States. With allotment, these policies paved the way for Euro-American settlement of the territory and thus for statehood. In 1907 Indian Territory and Oklahoma Territory combined to become the new state of Oklahoma.

These and other pressures on traditional culture were clear abrogations of tribal sovereignty, but tribes from the Southeast culture area saw just as clearly that fighting them head-on would prove unproductive. As a result, many engaged in passive resistance. Families refused to sign up for or receive their allotments. Former tribal council members revitalized traditional governance and ritual activities away from the geographic seats of power, and children were schooled at home. Ironically, the United States' efforts to complete the assimilation of the Southeastern peoples had resulted in a grassroots movement that strengthened traditional cultures considerably.

During the remainder of the 20th century, Southeastern peoples were affected by a number of events of global importance, such as the oil boom of the 1920s; the Great Depression; the World Wars and the Korean, Vietnam, and Gulf wars; and the advent of the civil rights and counterculture eras of the 1960s. In 1968 three Southeastern groups that had long been in bureaucratic limbo allied themselves to gain greater traction with the federal government. They included groups that had escaped removal—Cherokee communities in North Carolina and Seminole groups in Florida—as well as a tribelet of Choctaw that had traveled only as far as the state of Mississippi during removal. Having avoided removal and undertaken efforts to escape governmental scrutiny, they had seen many of their rights as native peoples abridged. Their efforts eventually led to federal recognition of their status as tribes.

During the 1970s the federal government relinquished the right to appoint tribal governments. The Southeastern tribes quickly reinstated their constitutions and held elections. From that point into the early 21st century, the Southeast nations emphasized economic development, the revenues of which were used to support programs ranging from education to health care to cultural preservation. For instance, Chickasaw Nation Industries and Choctaw Management Services Enterprise, each owned by its constituent tribe, included firms providing construction, information technology services, and professional recruiting. The Florida Seminole instituted ecotourism programs that acquainted visitors with the state's wetlands. Many tribes also turned to casino-based gaming. These operations often included hotel and restaurant facilities that generated income and provided employment to tribal members. Casino revenue, sometimes referred to as "the new buffalo," lifted many tribes above the poverty line and encouraged a revival of traditional cultural practices.

Chapter 6
SELECTED SOUTHEAST PEOPLES IN FOCUS

Even before they adopted practices of European settlers or acclimated to their new surroundings in the Indian Territory in what is now Oklahoma, the aboriginal peoples of the Southeast culture area had learned to adapt to a variety of climatic and environmental conditions. The southernmost portion of this culture area is coastal lowland that broadly encompasses the subtropical zone of southern Florida. Farther north, this gives way to the scrub forest, sandy soil, and savanna grassland of the coastal plains, as well as the alluvial floodplains of the Mississippi River. Moving inland, the piedmont dominates with a landscape of rolling hills and major river systems that is predominantly covered with forests of oak and hickory. A third zone is characterized by the portion of the Appalachian Mountains that lies in present-day eastern Tennessee, northern Georgia, and the western Carolinas, a land of high peaks, deeply etched valleys, hardwood forests, and, at high elevations, flora and fauna typical of more northerly regions.

Within this geographic range lived a number of tribes. A detailed discussion of the native societies of the Southeast culture area (in alphabetic order) follows.

APALACHEE

In the northwestern portion of present-day Florida, between the Aucilla and Apalachicola rivers, lived the Apalachee tribe. The Apalachee were a Muskogean-speaking people that inhabited the area above Apalachee

Bay. Their first encounters with Europeans occurred in the 16th century; the Spanish explorers Pánfilo de Narváez (in 1528) and Hernando de Soto (in 1539) led expeditions to Apalachee territory.

Traditionally, the tribe was divided into clans that traced descent through the maternal line. Chieftainship and office were hereditary, probably in the lineage within the clan. An agricultural people who cultivated maize (corn) and squash, the Apalachee were also noted warriors. They were ultimately subdued about 1600 and missionized by Spanish Franciscans. They continued to prosper (in 1655, 6,000–8,000 Apalachee occupied eight towns, each with a Franciscan mission) until early in the 18th century when Creek tribes to the north, incited by the British, began a series of raids on Apalachee settlements. These attacks culminated in 1703 when an army made up of a few hundred Englishmen and several thousand Creek warriors defeated the combined Spanish and Apalachee. The tribe was almost totally destroyed, and 1,400 Apalachee were removed to Carolina where some of them merged with the Creek. The remnants of the Florida tribe sought the protection of the French at Mobile and in Louisiana.

CADDO

Archaeological evidence uncovered in the lower Red River area of Louisiana and Arkansas indicates that this was land occupied for thousands of years by the Caddo, a single tribe within a confederacy composed of speakers of Caddoan languages. The Caddo got their name when the term *kadohadacho,* meaning "real chief" in their native language, was shortened by French settlers in the region. In the late 17th century they numbered approximately 8,000 persons living in villages scattered along the Red River

The grass huts of a Caddo village, as painted by William Langdon Kihn. These conical, thatched buildings typically surrounded sacred temple mounds. National Geographic Image Collection/The Bridgeman Art Library International

and its tributaries. This is also the region of the Caddoan archaeological complex, where many striking examples of workmanship have been found.

When first encountered by French and Spanish explorers, the Caddo were a semisedentary agricultural people. They lived in conical dwellings constructed of poles covered with a thatch of grass. These were grouped around ceremonial centres of temple mounds. The Caddo were skillful potters and basket makers. They wove cloth of vegetable fibres and, on special occasions, wore mantles decorated with feathers. They also wore nose rings and, like many other southeastern tribes, adorned their bodies with tattoos.

Traditional Caddo descent was matrilineal, and a hereditary upper group, marked by head flattening and other status symbols, directed political and religious activities. There are scattered reports of ceremonial human sacrifice and cannibalism. These and other traits probably indicate trade or other links between the Caddo and the centres of Aztec or Mayan cultures in Mexico and Yucatán.

During the 18th century the French and Spanish disputed over Caddo territory. The tribe was initially friendly to the French. By the close of the 18th century, colonial pressures had broken up Caddo tribal life and turned many of them into wanderers in their own land. When the vast territory of French Louisiana was purchased by the United States, the number of colonial settlers increased, and the tribe was pushed farther south. Under the treaty of 1835 the Caddo ceded all their land to the United States. The Louisiana Caddo moved southwest to join others of the tribe in Texas. There they lived peaceably for a time, but in 1859 threats of a massacre by a vigilante anti-Indian group forced them to flee to east-central Oklahoma, where they settled on a reservation on the banks of the Washita River.

Early 21st-century population estimates indicated more than 4,000 individuals of Caddo ancestry.

CALUSA

The Calusa inhabited the southwest coast of Florida from Tampa Bay to Cape Sable and Cape Florida, together with all the outlying keys. According to some authorities their territory also extended inland as far as Lake Okeechobee. Their linguistic affiliation is not certain. Their estimated population in 1650 was 3,000 living in 50 villages. The Calusa relied more on the sea than on agriculture for their livelihood. They made tools and weapons of seashells and fish bones. Their dwellings were of wood, built on piles, and their sacred buildings were erected on flat-topped mounds. They were fierce fighters and accomplished seamen, paddling their dugout canoes around the Florida coast. In their early period there is evidence of sacrifice of captives and of cannibalism.

KEY MARCO CARVINGS

The large group of carvings excavated at Key Marco in southern Florida provide the finest extant examples of North American Indian wood carving through the 15th century. The coastal mud of the area helped preserve hundreds of perishable artifacts, which were unearthed in 1896 during an excavation led by Smithsonian Institution–affiliated ethnographer Frank Hamilton Cushing. Among the artifacts found were painted wooden plaques, animal sculptures, human masks, nets, weights, and numerous tools. On the basis of radiocarbon dating, some of this material can be dated to the Late Woodland period (500–1000 CE), and it is believed to have been the work of the now-extinct Calusa Indians.

Especially notable among the artifacts are the highly realistic and sensitive animal carvings. These figures, presumed to have had a ceremonial use, retain traces of paint that once highlighted their sculptural form. Parts of these carvings, such as the ears of a deer, were originally hinged with leather to allow movement, and shell inlays were used for eyes. A 6-inch-high (15 cm) wooden feline figurine is the most famous of these objects. The degree of realism achieved in the carvings is unequaled in sculpture from the period produced north of Mexico, and some scholars have speculated—without evidence—that commerce might have gone on between the Indians of the Florida Keys and those of Mexico.

The Calusa also journeyed to Cuba and other Caribbean islands, trading in fish, skins, and amber. During the 16th century they defended their shores from a succession of Spanish explorers. Some research indicates that they may have immigrated to Cuba during the 18th century as a result of recurring invasions by the Creek and the English, while other work suggests they may have joined the Seminole, who moved into Florida early in the 19th century and were later removed to Oklahoma.

CATAWBA

The Catawba, who spoke a Siouan language, inhabited the territory around the Catawba River in what are now the states of North and South Carolina. Their principal village was on the west side of the river in north-central South Carolina. They were known among English colonial traders as Flatheads because, like a number of other tribes of the Southeast, they practiced ritual head flattening on male infants.

Traditional Catawba villages consisted of bark-covered cabins and a temple for public gatherings and religious ceremonies. Each village was governed by a council presided over by a chief. They subsisted principally by farming, harvesting two or more crops of maize (corn) each year and growing several varieties of beans, squash, and gourds. In most Southeast Indian cultures the farming was done by the women, but among the Catawba it was the men who farmed. A plentiful supply of passenger pigeons served as winter food. The Catawba made bowls, baskets, and mats, which they traded to other tribes and Europeans for meat and skins. Fish was also a staple of their diet. They caught sturgeon and herring using weirs, snares, and long poles.

In the 17th century the Catawba numbered about 5,000. As the Spanish, English, and French competed to colonize the Carolinas, the Catawba became virtual satellites of the various colonial factions. Their numbers fell off rapidly. In 1738 approximately half the tribe was wiped out in a smallpox epidemic, and by 1780 there were only an estimated 500 Catawba left. They were allies of the English in the Tuscarora War (1711–13) and in the French and Indian War (1754–63), but they aided the colonists in the American Revolution.

Early 21st-century population estimates indicated more than 2,500 Catawba descendants.

CHEROKEE

The Cherokee, of Iroquoian lineage, constituted one of the largest politically integrated tribes at the time of European colonization of the Americas. In 1650, some 22,500 Cherokee controlled approximately 40,000 square miles (100,000 square km) of the Appalachian Mountains in parts of present-day Georgia, eastern Tennessee, and the western Carolinas. Their name is derived from a Creek word meaning "people of different speech." Many prefer to be known by their self-names, Keetoowah or Tsalagi.

Traditional Cherokee life and culture greatly resembled that of the Creek and other tribes of the Southeast. The Cherokee nation was composed of a confederacy of symbolically red (war) and white (peace) towns. The chiefs of individual red towns were subordinated to a supreme war chief, while the officials of individual white towns were under the supreme peace chief. The peace towns provided sanctuary for wrongdoers. War ceremonies were conducted in red towns.

When encountered by Spanish explorers in the mid-16th century, the Cherokee possessed a variety of stone implements including knives, axes, and chisels. They wove baskets, made pottery, and cultivated maize (corn), beans, and squash. Deer, bear, and elk furnished meat and clothing. Cherokee dwellings were bark-roofed, windowless log cabins, with one door and a smoke hole in the roof. A typical Cherokee town had between 30 and 60 such houses and a council house, where general meetings were held and a sacred fire burned. An important religious observance was the Busk, or Green Corn Festival, a first-fruits and new-fires celebration.

The Spanish, French, and English all attempted to colonize parts of the Southeast, including Cherokee territory. By the early 18th century the tribe had chosen alliance with the British in both trading and military affairs. During the French and Indian War they allied themselves with the British. The French had allied themselves with several Iroquoian tribes that were the Cherokee's traditional enemies. By 1759 the British had begun to engage in a scorched-earth policy that led to the indiscriminate destruction of native towns, including those of the Cherokee and other British-allied tribes. Tribal economies were seriously disrupted by British actions. In 1773 the Cherokee and Creek had to exchange a portion of their land to relieve the resulting indebtedness, ceding more than two million acres in Georgia through the Treaty of Augusta.

In 1775 the Overhill Cherokee were persuaded at the Treaty of Sycamore Shoals to sell an enormous tract of land in central Kentucky to the privately owned Transylvania Land Company. Although land sales to private companies violated British law, the treaty nevertheless became the basis for the colonial settlement of that area. As the American War of Independence loomed, the Transylvania Land Company declared its support of the revolutionaries; the Cherokee became convinced that the British were more likely to enforce boundary laws than a new government and announced their determination to support the crown. Despite British attempts to restrain them, a force of 700 Cherokee under Chief Dragging Canoe attacked the colonist-held forts of Eaton's Station and Fort Watauga (in what is now North Carolina) in July 1776. Both assaults failed, and the tribe retreated in disgrace. These raids were the first in a series of attacks by Cherokee, Creek, and Choctaw on frontier towns, eliciting a vigorous response by militia and regulars of the Southern colonies during September and October. At the end of this time, Cherokee power was broken, their crops and villages destroyed, and their warriors dispersed. The defeated tribes sued for peace. In order to obtain it, they were forced to surrender vast tracts of territory in North and South Carolina at the Treaty of DeWitt's Corner (May 20, 1777) and the Treaty of Long Island of Holston (July 20, 1777).

Peace reigned for the next two years. When Cherokee raids flared up in 1780 during the American preoccupation with British armed forces elsewhere, punitive action led by Col. Arthur Campbell and Col. John Sevier subdued the tribe again. The second Treaty of Long Island of Holston (July 26, 1781) confirmed previous land cessions and caused the Cherokee to yield additional territory.

After 1800 the Cherokee were remarkable for their assimilation of American settler culture. The tribe formed a government modeled on that of the United States. Under Chief Junaluska they aided Andrew Jackson against the Creek in the Creek War, particularly in the Battle of Horseshoe Bend. They adopted colonial methods of farming, weaving, and home building. Perhaps most remarkable of all was the syllabary of the Cherokee language, developed in 1821 by Sequoyah, a Cherokee who had served with the U.S. Army in the Creek War. The syllabary—a system of writing in which each symbol represents a syllable—was so successful that almost the entire tribe became literate within a short time. A written constitution was adopted, and religious literature flourished, including translations from the Christian Scriptures. Native Americans' first newspaper, the *Cherokee Phoenix*, began publication in February 1828.

SEQUOYAH

(b. c. 1776, Taskigi, North Carolina colony [U.S.]—d. August 1843, near San Fernando, Mex.)

The creator of the Cherokee writing system was Sequoyah (also spelled Sequoya or Sequoia). The Cherokee version of his name is Sikwayi. He was probably the son of a Virginia fur trader named Nathaniel Gist, for which reason he is also called George Gist. Reared in the Tennessee country by his Cherokee mother, Wuhteh of the Paint clan, he never learned to speak, read, or write English. He was an accomplished silversmith, painter, and warrior and served with the U.S. Army in the Creek War in 1813–14.

Sequoyah became convinced that the secret of what he considered the white people's superior power was written language, which enabled them to accumulate and transmit more

Sequoyah. Library of Congress Prints and Photographs Division, Washington, D.C. 20540

knowledge than was possible for a people dependent on memory and word of mouth. Accordingly, about 1809 he began working to develop a system of writing for the Cherokee, believing that increased knowledge would help them maintain their independence from the whites. He experimented first with pictographs and then with symbols representing the syllables of the spoken Cherokee language, adapting letters from English, Greek, and Hebrew. His daughter helped him to identify the Cherokee syllables. By 1821 he had created a system of 86 symbols, representing all the syllables of the Cherokee language.

Sequoyah convinced his people of the utility of his syllabary by transmitting messages between the Cherokee of Arkansas (with whom he went to live) and those of the east and by teaching his daughter and other young people of the tribe to write. The simplicity of his system enabled pupils to learn it rapidly, and soon Cherokee throughout the nation were teaching it in their schools and publishing books and newspapers in their own Cherokee language.

One spelling of his name, Sequoia, was used for the genus of the giant redwoods (*Sequoia sempervirens*) of the Pacific Coast and the big trees (*Sequoiadendron giganteum*) of the Sierra Nevada range.

The Cherokee's rapid acquisition of settler culture did not protect them against the land hunger of those they emulated. When gold was discovered on Cherokee land in Georgia, agitation for the removal of the tribe increased. In December 1835 the Treaty of New Echota, signed by a small minority of the Cherokee, ceded to the United States all Cherokee land east of the Mississippi River for $5 million. The overwhelming majority of tribal members repudiated the treaty and took their case to the U.S. Supreme Court. The Court rendered a decision favourable to the tribe, declaring that Georgia had no jurisdiction over the Cherokee and no claim to their land.

Georgia officials ignored the Court's decision, President Andrew Jackson refused to enforce it, and Congress passed the Indian Removal Act of 1830 to facilitate the eviction of tribal members from their homes and territory. Removal was implemented by 7,000 troops commanded by Gen. Winfield Scott. Scott's men moved through Cherokee territory, forcing many people from their homes at gunpoint. As many as 15,000 Cherokee were thus gathered into camps while their homes were plundered and burned by local residents. Subsequently these refugees were sent west in groups of about 1,000, the majority on foot.

The eviction and forced march, which came to be known as the Trail of Tears, took place during the fall and winter of 1838–39. Although Congress had allocated funds for the operation, it was badly mismanaged, and inadequate food supplies, shelter, and clothing led to terrible suffering, especially after frigid weather arrived. About 4,000 Cherokee died on the 116-day journey, many because the escorting troops refused to slow or stop so that the ill and exhausted could recover.

When the main body had finally reached its new home in what is now northeastern Oklahoma, new controversies began with the settlers already there. Feuds and murders rent the tribe as reprisals were made on those who had signed the Treaty of New Echota.

In Oklahoma the Cherokee joined four other tribes — the Creek, Chickasaw, Choctaw, and Seminole — all of which had been forcibly removed from the Southeast by the U.S. government in the 1830s. For three-quarters of a century, each tribe had a land allotment and a quasi-autonomous government modeled on that of the United States. In preparation for Oklahoma statehood (1907), some of this land was allotted to individual tribal members. The rest was opened up to homesteaders, held in trust by the federal government, or allotted to freed slaves. Tribal governments were effectively dissolved in 1906 but have continued to exist in a limited form.

At the time of removal in 1838, a few hundred individuals escaped to the mountains and furnished the nucleus for the several thousand Cherokee who were living in western North Carolina in the 21st century. Early 21st-century population estimates indicated more than 730,000 individuals of Cherokee descent living across the United States.

CHICKASAW

The Chickasaw originally inhabited what is now northern Mississippi and Alabama. At one point early in their history, the Muskogean-speaking Chickasaw may have been joined with the Choctaw to form a single tribe. Traditionally, the Chickasaw were a seminomadic people who patrolled the immense territory that they claimed for themselves and raided tribes far to the north. Like many conquering peoples, they integrated the remnants of these tribes into their culture.

Descent among the Chickasaw was matrilineal. Originally the tribe's dwellings were spread out along streams and rivers, rather than clustered together in villages. The supreme deity was associated with the sky, sun, and fire; a harvest and new-fire rite similar to the Green Corn ceremony of the Creek was celebrated annually.

Probably the earliest contact between Europeans and the Chickasaw was Hernando de Soto's expedition in 1540–41. In the 18th century the Chickasaw became involved in the power struggles between the British and French, siding with the British against the French and the Choctaw. They also gave refuge to the Natchez in their wars with the French. Relations with the United States began in 1786, when their northern territorial boundary was fixed at the Ohio River.

In the 1830s they were forcibly removed to Indian Territory (present day Oklahoma) where, with the Creek, Cherokee, Choctaw, and Seminole, they were among the Five Civilized Tribes. Over the remainder of the 19th century and into the 20th, the Chickasaw and other tribes were able to exercise a certain amount of self-governance within the boundaries of land allotted to them by the U.S. government. As Oklahoma approached statehood in 1907, however, a large portion of the Indian Territory was parceled off to homesteaders and freed slaves, or simply held in trust by the federal government. Subsequently, the authority and sanctity of tribal governments were greatly diminished. Some Chickasaw now live on tribal landholdings that are informally called reservations.

Early estimates placed the tribe's population at 3,000–4,000. At the time of their removal to Indian Territory they numbered about 5,000. Chickasaw descendants numbered more than 38,000 in the early 21st century.

CHOCTAW

The Choctaw traditionally lived in what is now southeastern Mississippi. Choctaw is a Muskogean dialect quite similar to that of the Chickasaw, and, as mentioned previously, there is evidence that they are a branch of the latter tribe. In the mid-18th century, some 20,000 Choctaw lived in thatched-roofed log and bark cabins within 60 or 70 settlements located along the Pearl, Chickasawhay, and Pascagoula rivers. Skillful farmers, the Choctaw produced surplus crops, including corn, beans, and pumpkins, to sell and trade. For sustenance they also fished, gathered nuts and wild fruits, and hunted deer and bear.

The most important Choctaw community ritual was the Busk, or Green Corn, Festival, a first-fruits and new-fire rite celebrated at midsummer. A notable funerary custom involved the ritual removal of the bones of the deceased from the body. Subsequently, the bones were placed in an ossuary. This ritual was performed by spiritually powerful men and women known as bone-gatherers or bone-pickers, with the departed's family members in attendance. Bone-gatherers were notable for their distinctive tattooing and long fingernails.

In the power struggles that took place after colonization, the Choctaw were generally allied with the French against the English, the Chickasaw, and other Native American tribes. After the French defeat in the French and Indian War (1754–63), some Choctaw land was ceded to the United States and some tribal members began moving west across the Mississippi. In the 19th century the growth of the European market for cotton increased the pressure for the acquisition of Choctaw land, and in 1820 they ceded 5,000,000 acres in west central Mississippi to the United States. In the 1830s the Choctaw were forced to move to what is now Oklahoma, as were the other members of the Five Civilized Tribes—the Creek, Cherokee, Chickasaw, and Seminole. Each of these tribes established a government patterned after the U.S. federal government, and enjoyed at least partial autonomy. The granting of statehood to Oklahoma, however, severely limited the sovereignty of the Choctaw and other native peoples once again. Land that had been granted to the tribes was offered to homesteaders headed to the new state, allotted to freed slaves, or held in trust by the U.S. government. The authority of the tribal governments was thus undercut, and they were largely dissolved by 1906. Choctaw descendants numbered more than 159,000 in the early 21st century.

CREEK

A large section of Georgia and Alabama flatlands was originally controlled by the Creek. The Muskogee (or Upper Creek) settled the northern Creek territory while the Hitchiti and Alabama, who had the same general traditions as the Upper Creek but spoke a slightly different Muskogean dialect, occupied the lower territories.

Traditional Creek economy was based primarily on agriculture. Creek farmers cultivated maize (corn), beans, and squash. Most of the farming was done by women, while the men of the tribe were responsible for hunting and defense. The Creek achieved status based on individual merit rather than by inheriting it. Like most Indians of the Southeast, they commonly tattooed their entire bodies.

Before colonization, Creek towns were symbolically grouped into white and red categories, set apart for peace ceremonials and war ceremonials, respectively. Each town had a plaza or community square, around which were grouped the houses — rectangular structures with four vertical walls of poles plastered over with mud to form wattle. The roofs were pitched and covered with either bark or thatch, with smoke holes left open at the gables. If the town had a temple, it was a thatched dome-shaped edifice set upon an eight-foot (2.4 m) mound into which stairs were cut to the temple door. The plaza was the gathering point for such important religious observances as the Busk, or Green Corn, ceremony, an annual first-fruits and new-fire rite. A distinctive feature of this midsummer festival was that every wrongdoing, grievance, or crime — short of murder — was forgiven.

The Creek first made contact with Europeans in 1538 when Hernando de Soto invaded their territory. Subsequently, the Creek allied themselves with the English colonists in a succession of wars (beginning about

1703) against the Apalachee and the Spanish. During the 18th century, a Creek Confederacy was organized in an attempt to present a united front against both native and white enemies. It comprised not only the dominant Creek but also speakers of other Muskogean languages (Hitchiti, Alabama-Koasati) and of non-Muskogean languages (Yuchi, some Natchez and Shawnee). The Seminole of Florida and Oklahoma are a branch of the Creek Confederacy of the 18th and early 19th centuries.

Ultimately, the confederacy did not succeed, in part because the Creek towns (about 50 with a total population of perhaps 20,000) were not able to coordinate the contribution of warriors to a common battle. In 1813–14, when the Creek War with the United States took place, some towns fought with the white colonizers and some (the Red Sticks) against them. Upon defeat, the Creek ceded 23 million acres of land (half of Alabama and part of southern Georgia). They were forcibly removed to Indian Territory (now Oklahoma) in the 1830s. There with the Cherokee, Chickasaw, Choctaw, and Seminole, they constituted one of the Five Civilized Tribes. Each of the tribes was able to establish its own government, which gave them some semblance of sovereignty. However, much of the land allotted to the Creek and the other four tribes was made available for homesteading in anticipation of Oklahoma's impending statehood in 1907. Other parcels were granted to freed slaves or held in reserve by the federal government. By 1906, tribal governments that had been in operation for nearly three-quarters of a century effectively ceased to exist. Creek descendants numbered more than 71,000 in the early 21st century.

NATCHEZ

The east side of the lower Mississippi River was home to the Natchez, which were part of the Algonquian language family. The early Natchez economy relied primarily on maize (corn) agriculture. They made clothes by weaving a fabric from the inner bark of the mulberry and excelled in pottery production. Like several other groups of Southeast Indians, the Natchez built substantial earthen mounds as foundations for large wattle-and-daub temple structures. Their dwellings—built in precise rows around a plaza or common ground—were also constructed of wattle and daub and had arched cane roofs.

Traditional Natchez religion venerated the sun, which was represented by a perpetual fire kept burning in a temple. All fires in a village, including the sacred fire, were allowed to die once a year on the eve of the midsummer Green Corn ceremony, or Busk. The sacred fire was remade at dawn of the festival day, and all the village hearths were then lit anew from the sacred flames.

Natchez social organization was notable for its caste system. The system drew from and supported Natchez religious beliefs and classified individuals as suns, nobles, honoured people, and commoners. Persons of the sun caste were required to marry commoners. The offspring of female suns and commoners were suns, while the children of male suns and commoners belonged to the caste of honoured people. The heads of villages also claimed descent from the sun, and the monarch was referred to as the Great Sun. He was entitled to marry several wives and to maintain servants. Upon his death his wives and some servants, along with any others who wished to join him in the afterlife, were ritually sacrificed.

Historians estimate that approximately 6,000 Natchez individuals, living in a handful of villages located between the Yazoo and Pearl rivers in Mississippi, were on hand to greet French colonizers when they arrived in the early 18th century. Relations between the French and the Natchez were friendly at first, but three French-Natchez wars—in 1716, 1723, and 1729—resulted in the French, with the aid of the Choctaw, driving the Natchez from their villages. In 1731 some 400 Natchez were captured and sold into the West Indian slave trade. The remainder took refuge with the Chickasaw and later with the Upper Creek and Cherokee. When the latter tribes were forced to move west into Indian Territory (Oklahoma), the Natchez went with them.

Early 21st-century population estimates indicated some 500 individuals of Natchez descent.

SEMINOLE

The Seminole are of Creek origin. The Seminole tribe was formed when migrant Creek relocated from towns in southern Georgia to north Florida locations as the 18th century wound to a close. Their name, which dates back to 1775, reflects their history; Seminole is believed to be derived from the Creek word *simanó-li*, meaning "separatist," or "runaway." The name may also have been a permutation of the Spanish word *cimarrón*, meaning "wild."

The Seminole were not the only peoples that sought refuge in isolated villages built amid the dense patchwork of thickets and wetlands known as the Florida Everglades. Escaped African, African American, and Native American slaves were welcomed by the tribe, as were other individuals attempting to avoid the bloody power struggles between European colonizers and other Southeast Indians.

The Seminole economy emphasized hunting, fishing, and gathering wild foods. They also grew maize (corn) and other produce on high ground within the wetlands. Homes included substantial log cabins and, later, thatched-roof shelters with open sides known as "chickees." People typically wore long tunics. By the late 19th century, Seminole clothing was often decorated with brightly coloured strips of cloth.

The Seminole chief Osceola, who led his people in battle against the U.S. government during the Second Seminole War. MPI/Archive Photos/ Getty Images

In an effort to stem further colonial encroachment and to avoid forced removal to the west, the Seminole fought a succession of wars in 1817–18, 1835–42, and 1855–58. As a result of the First Seminole War, Spain ceded its Florida holdings to the United States. In 1832 a treaty proposal that would have obligated the Seminole to move west of the Mississippi River was rejected by a large portion of the tribe. The Second Seminole War was one of the most costly of the U.S.-Indian wars, with military expenditures of tens of millions of dollars. In 1838 the Seminole chief Osceola and other tribal leaders agreed to meet the U.S. military under a flag of truce. The American forces broke the truce by imprisoning the men, and Osceola died in custody some three months later. Fighting continued sporadically for another four years, but the tribe eventually surrendered. The people were required to move to Indian Territory (Oklahoma) and were resettled in the western part of the Creek reservation there. A few Seminole remained in Florida.

In Oklahoma the Seminole became one of the Five Civilized Tribes, which also included the Cherokee, Chickasaw, Creek, and Choctaw, all of whom had been forcibly removed from the southeastern United States by the federal government in the 1830s. Land allotted to each of the five tribes was subject to quasi-autonomous forms of government established by the tribes themselves and modeled after the U.S. federal government. Oklahoma being made a state in 1907 disrupted the Seminole's way of life once again. While some land was allotted to individual tribe members, large portions of the territory were opened to homesteaders or granted to freed slaves. Land loss led to diminished sovereignty; tribal governments had all but dissolved by 1906. Changes in these federal policies resulted in the revitalization of the tribal governments in the mid-20th century.

SEMINOLE WARS

Three conflicts known as the Seminole Wars were fought between the United States and the Seminole Indians of Florida in the period before the American Civil War. These wars ultimately resulted in the opening of the Seminole land for white exploitation and settlement.

The First Seminole War (1817–18) began over attempts by U.S. authorities to recapture runaway black slaves living among Seminole bands. Under General Andrew Jackson, U.S. military forces invaded the area, scattering the villagers, burning their towns, and seizing Spanish-held Pensacola and St. Marks. The international upshot of this war was that Spain was induced in 1819 to cede its Florida territory under the terms of the Transcontinental Treaty.

The Second Seminole War (1835–42) followed the refusal of most Seminole to abandon the reservation that had been specifically established for them north of Lake Okeechobee and to relocate west of the Mississippi River. Whites coveted this land and sought to oust the Seminole under the Indian Removal Act. Led by their dynamic chief Osceola, the Seminole warriors hid their families in the swamp lands of the Everglades and fought vigorously to defend their homeland, using guerrilla tactics. As many as 2,000 U.S. soldiers were killed in this prolonged fighting, which cost the government tens of millions of dollars. Only after Osceola's capture while parleying under a flag of truce did Indian resistance decline. With peace, most Seminole agreed to emigrate.

The Third Seminole War (1855–58) resulted from renewed efforts to track down the Seminole remnant remaining in Florida. It caused little bloodshed and ended with the United States paying the most resistant band of refugees to go West.

For some 40 years, those Seminole who stayed in Florida endured hardships related to their resistance to removal. By the close of the 19th century, however, relations with neighbouring Euro-Americans had improved.

During the first half of the 20th century, tribal members regained some 80,000 acres of land from the U.S. government. In 1957, a century after the end of the Seminole Wars, the Seminole tribe of Florida regained federal recognition. Over the next 50 years the tribe developed economic programs ranging from citrus production to tourist attractions and infrastructure, including an eco-tourism park, a tribal museum, a casino, and a private airstrip.

Early 21st-century population estimates indicated some 27,000 individuals of Seminole descent.

TIMUCUA

Timucua is a term used to describe the Native Americans who inhabited the northeast coast of present-day Florida, as well as the language these individuals spoke. By the mid-17th century an estimated 13,000 Timucua speakers lived in the area; 8,000 of those spoke Timucua proper while the remainder were fluent in various sister tongues. The explorer Ponce de León and his crew were believed to be the first Europeans to come in contact with the Timucua, in the 16th century. Later these indigenous peoples were missionized by the Franciscans, who compiled a grammar of the Timucua language.

In the early 1700s Timucua territory was invaded by the Creek Indians and the English. As a result of these incursions, many Timucua died in armed conflict, perished from deprivation, or succumbed to Old World diseases to which they had no immunity. Sometime after 1736 the remnants of the tribe moved to the area near the present Mosquito Lagoon in Florida. It is likely that the remaining Timucua were eventually absorbed into Seminole culture.

TUSCARORA

When first encountered by Europeans in the 17th century, the Iroquoian-speaking Tuscarora occupied what is now North Carolina. They were noted for their use of indigenous hemp for fibre and medicine. Their name derives from an Iroquoian term meaning "hemp gatherers."

Traditionally, the Tuscarora depended heavily on cultivating maize (corn). They were also expert hunters. Later they expanded their economy by trading rum to neighbouring Indian groups. The typical Tuscarora dwelling was a round lodge of poles overlaid with bark. Evidence suggests that they were organized in exogamous clans, with the clans grouped into two moieties in each of the three tribes constituting the Tuscarora nation.

After the British established trade in the area (*c.* 1670), they frequently kidnapped Tuscarora men, women, and children to be sold into slavery. British traders also seized tribal lands without payment. These depredations led to the outbreak of war in 1711, after Tuscarora attempts to obtain relief peacefully were repulsed. Over the following 90 years the Tuscarora moved northward, having been admitted into the Iroquois Confederacy as the sixth nation. Many Tuscarora supported the revolutionaries in the American War of Independence. Those who favoured the British were granted lands on Grand River reservation, in Ontario. The highest estimate of Tuscarora population in the early 17th century was about 5,000. Tuscarora descendants numbered more than 5,600 in the early 21st century.

Native Americans of the Northeast and Southeast are sometimes considered together as a culture area known as the Eastern Woodlands. This classification is made possible because of a lack of sharply defined geographic boundaries between the two regions. In the early days of European colonization, traditions and practices of Northeastern tribes filtered down into and were adopted by Southeastern societies, reinforcing the bonds between the two culture areas.

Yet the Northeast and the Southeast are distinct, unique areas of indigenous culture. Language families, kinship, climate, and physical environment are the biggest factors that separate one area from the other. Centuries of European incursion altered Native American life in these regions. But members of the affected tribes fought to retain many of their traditions and practices despite enforced relocation and attempted assimilation. Pride in their culture is as important to 21st-century Native Americans of the Northeast and Southeast as it was to their ancestors long ago.

aboriginal Being the first or the earliest of its kind in a particular region.

acculturation The process of changes in customs and beliefs from one culture to another, either voluntarily or as the result of being vanquished.

animism The belief that all things—animate or otherwise—have a living essence and are capable of either harming or helping human beings.

assimilation The process by which individuals or groups of a particular ethnic heritage are "mainstreamed" into a society's prevalent culture.

band A small, egalitarian, family-based group of people. In the context of this book, a band is one of several subdivisions of a tribe.

breechcloth A soft leather strip drawn between the legs and held in place by securing at the waist with a belt.

calumet A ceremonial tobacco pipe, known colloquially as a "peace pipe."

culture area The anthropological term for a geographic region in which the inhabitants share many societal traits.

dugout A boat made from a single hollowed-out log.

exogamous Used to describe a marriage outside of one's own group or culture.

indigenous Having originated in, or being the first to occupy, a particular area or region.

levirate A custom in which a man weds his dead brother's widow and takes on the responsibility of providing for her and her children.

longhouse A long, rectangular domicile favoured by indigenous peoples of the American Northeast.

matrilineal Based on the mother's heritage and familial lines.

moiety A tribal subdivision that has a complementary counterpart.

patrilineal Based on the father's heritage and familial lines.

polygyny A form of marriage in which two or more wives share a husband.

shaman A man or woman who has shown an exceptionally strong affinity with the spirit world. Shamans are also considered healers and are thought to be adept at divination.

subsistence A way of behaving that ensures survival.

syllabary A system of writing in which each symbol represents a syllable.

syncretic Fusing two or more traditions.

tribe A large group that shares traditions, lineage, language, or ideology. Native American tribes are made up of smaller, semi-independent groups called bands that share some of these features.

vision quest A supernatural experience in which an individual seeks to interact with a guardian spirit, usually an anthropomorphized animal, to obtain advice or protection.

wampum Beaded strings or belts made from polished shells, which served as money for some Native American tribes.

wattle A building cover comprised of poles through which reeds or branches have been woven.

wickiup A dome-shaped form of lodging favoured by Northeastern Native American tribes, constructed by draping bent samplings with rushes, grass, bark, or the like.

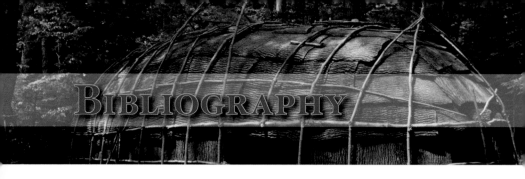

Few sources treat both the Northeast and the Southeast culture areas together. Those that do tend to include other culture areas as well and to discuss broad topics, such as art or archaeology. A good general background is provided by such sources as Barry Pritzker, *A Native American Encyclopedia: History, Culture, and Peoples* (2000); and Jordan D. Paper, *Native North American Religious Traditions: Dancing for Life* (2007).

THE NORTHEAST PEOPLES

Regional syntheses of the traditional cultures of the Northeast are in Robert E. Ritzenthaler and Pat Ritzenthaler, *The Woodland Indians of the Western Great Lakes* (1970, reissued 1991); Howard S. Russell, *Indian New England Before the Mayflower* (1980); Bruce G. Trigger, *Natives and Newcomers: Canada's "Heroic Age" Reconsidered* (1985), covering the period from 9000 BCE to the mid-19th century; William C. Sturtevant (ed.), *Handbook of North American Indians*, vol. 15, Northeast, ed. by Bruce Trigger (1978); and Kathleen J. Bragdon, *The Columbia Guide to American Indians of the Northeast* (2001, reissued 2005).

General discussions of the historical period include Neal Salisbury, *Manitou and Providence: Indians, Europeans, and the Making of New England, 1500–1643* (1982); Alden T. Vaughan, *New England Frontier: Puritans and Indians, 1620–1675*, rev. ed. (1979); W.

Vernon Kinietz, *The Indians of the Western Great Lakes, 1615–1760* (1940, reissued 1991); Francis Jennings, *The Ambiguous Iroquois Empire* (1984), on the period from the early 1600s to 1744; Helen Hornbeck Tanner et al. (eds.), *Atlas of Great Lakes Indian History* (1987), with an extensive bibliography; Richard White, *The Middle Ground: Indians, Empires, and Republics in the Great Lakes Region, 1650–1815* (1991); Daniel K. Richter, *The Ordeal of the Longhouse: The Peoples of the Iroquois League in the Era of European Colonization* (1992); Kathleen J. Bragdon, *Native People of Southern New England, 1500–1650* (1996); Colin G. Calloway, *After King Philip's War: Presence and Persistence in Indian New England* (1997). Also of interest are Guy Chet, *Conquering the American Wilderness: The Triumph of European Warfare in the Colonial Northeast* (2003); Jordan E. Kerber (ed.), *Cross-Cultural Collaboration: Native Peoples and Archaeology in the Northeastern United States* (2006), an anthology of essays; Lisa Tanya Brooks, *The Common Pot: The Recovery of Native Space in the Northeast* (2008); and Mary Ann Levine, Kenneth E. Sassaman, and Michael S. Nassaney (eds.), *The Archaeological Northeast* (2000).

THE SOUTHEAST PEOPLES

Regional syntheses of the traditional cultures of the Southeast are in Fred B. Kniffen, Hiram F. Gregory, and George A. Stokes, *The Historic Indian Tribes of Louisiana: From 1542 to the Present* (1987); Charles Hudson, *The Southeastern Indians* (1976, reissued 1992); Theda Perdue and Michael D. Green, *The Columbia Guide to American Indians of the Southeast* (2001); and William C. Sturtevant (ed.), *Handbook of North American Indians*, vol. 14, Southeast, ed. by Raymond D. Fogelson (2004).

Discussions of particular historical periods include Verner W. Crane, *The Southern Frontier, 1670–1732* (1929, reissued 1981); R.S. Cotterill, *The Southern Indians: The Story of the Civilized Tribes Before Removal* (1954, reissued 1983); William G. McLoughlin, *Cherokee Renascence in the New Republic* (1986, reissued 1992), a history of relations between the Cherokee and Euro-Americans, 1789–1833; James H. Merrell, *The Indians' New World: Catawbas and Their Neighbors from European Contact Through the Era of Removal* (1989); Joel W. Martin, *Sacred Revolt: The Muskogees' Struggle for a New World* (1991), covering the period from the 17th to the early 19th century; and Michelene E. Pesantubbee, *Choctaw Women in a Chaotic World: The Clash of Cultures in the Colonial Southeast* (2005), a text that explores the roles of Choctaw women from the contact period through the 20th century.

The profound impact of removal on the Southeastern tribes is illuminated in a variety of works, including Grant Foreman, *The Five Civilized Tribes* (1934, reissued 1989), and *Indian Removal: The Emigration of the Five Civilized Tribes of Indians*, new ed. (1972, reissued 1989); Angie Debo, *And Still the Waters Run* (1940, reprinted 1984); Walter L. Williams (ed.), *Southeastern Indians Since the Removal Era* (1979); J. Leitch Wright, Jr., *The Only Land They Knew: The Tragic Story of the American Indians in the Old South* (1981); Samuel J. Wells and Roseanna Tubby (eds.), *After Removal: The Choctaw in Mississippi* (1986); James H. Howard and Willie Lena, *Oklahoma Seminoles: Medicines, Magic, and Religion* (1984); Thurman Wilkins, *Cherokee Tragedy*, 2nd ed. rev. (1986); and William L. Anderson (ed.), *Cherokee Removal: Before and After* (1991), a collection of interdisciplinary essays.

INDEX